# The P.R.I.D.E. Factor

## How To Bounce Back When You Think You Can't

by

## Carol Ann Munschauer, Ph. D. and Dave Hood

authorHOUSE

*1663 LIBERTY DRIVE, SUITE 200*
*BLOOMINGTON, INDIANA 47403*
*(800) 839-8640*
*www.authorhouse.com*

First published by AuthorHouse 10/27/04

ISBN: 1-4184-8350-8 (sc)
ISBN: 1-4184-8351-6 (dj)

Printed in the United States of America
Bloomington, Indiana

This book is printed on acid-free paper.

# Contents

# Here's What The Experts Are Saying About The P.R.I.D.E. Factor

This book has helped me make great strides in the problem I have had with my need for perfection. I was always accommodating to the needs of others and, as a result, I suffered undue stress, shame and anxiety whenever I disappointed anyone. Reading the cases in the book, and learning the principles of the P.R.I.D.E. Factor, released me from the curse of always feeling bad about myself whenever I followed my own ideas. It gave me the emotional independence I needed to be my True Self. My "step is lighter" and I am not so hard on myself. People close to me can see the difference.

Christian Phoenix
Special Education Teacher

The P.R.I.D.E. Factor offers the reader a chance to become free of the bondage associated with pain, hurt and suffering. I have seen, first hand, in my work as a priest, counselor and law enforcement chaplain that the principles of this book work. I have been deep in the pit of Ground Zero. I have been steeped in the fear and terror of Emergency Rooms. I have often been called to people's homes to intervene in a crisis such as trying to prevent a potential suicide, helping a family bear some unbearable grief, or trying to move them through some other emotional pain from which they could picture no light at the end of their dark tunnel. The tools I learned in this book gave me new ways of healing to add to my armamentarium, especially in dealing with people's shame and guilt. One of the most vivid examples emblazoned in my memory is having been able to release a firefighter from his guilt and shame in his final hours as he was pinned under debris. The principles in this book can truly be life giving; as a life, no matter how long it is, lived buried in shame and guilt, is no life at all.

Father Joe Moreno
World Trade Center/Ground Zero Chaplain

I want to say what an achievement I think this book is. It is a captivating blend of contemporary psychoanalytic thought and issues about resilience that concern us all today. It is rich with stories and examples of adults who have "bounced back" despite the odds, and guidance for parents on how to raise children who are prepared to do so in their own lives. I think that all parents would find the book inspirational. The book is also presented in a clear, engaging and upbeat tone. Although it is rich with sound information, it is presented in language that is easily understandable and accessible to the layperson. I, myself, have had formal training in these concepts and have treated both adults and children who faced the challenge of "bouncing back." Having words that lay people can also understand and work with is a real contribution. But mostly what I loved about the book is that it made me happy!

Margot Garfield LICSW
( Licensed Independent Clinical Social Worker ),
M. Ed, Advanced Candidate in Psychoanalysis

As a Superior of a religious community, I found that the focus on resilience and the capacity to "bounce back" are essential both for the psychological health of the individual and also for the well being of a community. The principles presented in this book have helped me manage many difficult human situations with increased confidence.

Fr. Patrick  Lynch

S.J. Rector of Canisius  College Jesuit Community

*To my father, Fred Munschauer Jr., who is my inspiration – his love and enthusiasms*
*have always risen victorious over the setbacks of life.*

*CM*

*To my parents, Richard & Virginia Hood, without whose wise guidance*
*and love I could not have achieved my goals.*
*To my wife, Rebecca, whose support, love and enthusiasm*
*makes every day a grand adventure.*

*DH*

# ACKNOWLEDGMENTS

First of all I thank the people who have made me who I am. I am grateful to all who have given me the nourishment I have needed to develop and maintain my goals, enthusiasms and discipline. These are the people who have let me come close into their lives and to enter into their True Selves. You will see glimpses of some of these people in this book.

I am especially indebted to my mother, Harriet, my father, Fred, my brother, Rick and my Uncle Donald and Aunt Marion Swenson, who have always encouraged me to follow my own path, even when they, at times, felt generally bewildered by its direction. I also thank everyone who has been supportive to me (currently) as I have worked on this project; and the people I know I will be able to count on to be supportive to me in the future as the **P.R.I.D.E. Factor**™ takes on a life of its own.

I thank the people who have given me the privilege of being their doctor. They have enriched my life by letting me learn about how they have managed to bounce back when they never thought that they could. It is impossible to be so close to such people without developing a deep affection for them, and, at times, even love. You know who you are, and I thank you all for so deeply touching my being. I thank you for what I have learned from you and I thank you for contributing your ideas to this book, both directly and indirectly.

I also want to thank my son, Grant Munschauer Pearson, who came to my husband and me later in life than we had wished, but whose existence and essence has given me vitality beyond belief. Were it not for him, I would never have become an expert on big vehicles and would never have encountered Dave Hood and his movies in the first place.

I want to thank my husband, Paul Pearson, who so generously allowed me to immerse myself in soothing Grant all night long during his years of interrupted sleep, and who gave me the space on many, many weekends to seclude myself in my office to work on this book. This book's contribution came at a great expense to his comfort, and I thank him from the bottom of my heart for this. He, along with my closest family and friends, will always be cherished the most for the love and backing they gave me during the numerous heartbreaking defeats we suffered during our ten years of high-tech infertility treatments. This is where I first learned, very personally, about the essential need for a responsive support network if one is ever going to be able to bounce back. After crushing disappointments and all too many miscarriages, in the end, it was the precepts of the **P.R.I.D.E. Factor**™ that enabled us to get through.

I want to thank Dr. Alexander Golbin for diagnosing Grant's sleep disorder and giving it legitimacy. His expertise and compassion helped Grant and me to be able to "ride it through" together during seemingly interminable nights of disrupted sleep. In this context, I also want to thank my friend and colleague Dr. Malcolm Slavin for urging me to stay with Grant all night and to "use my body" to comfort him during his sleepless nights.

I also want to give special thanks to Dr. Howard Bacal, for his sustained belief in me, and his contribution of Specificity Theory, which advocates a mother's tailoring her response, within her own capacity, to the needs of her individual child. Both of these contributions serve as ballast for me during many turbulent nights. I also give thanks to Dr. Joseph Lichtenberg, Dr. James Fosshage and Dr. William and Martha Sears for supporting me in this up-close approach which would have been controversial to other theorists.

I also want to thank my longtime friend and mentor Dr. Andrew Morrison for teaching me most of what I know about the emotion of shame and for re-introducing the whole field of contemporary psychoanalysis to the destructiveness of this feeling for both children and adults. It is the enlightenment he gave to the field of psychoanalysis that heightened my attunement to much of what Dave was conveying beneath the surface of his stories; all of us who love children have Andy to thank for this.

I also want to acknowledge noted dream researcher and theorist Dr. Harry Hunt, who provided me with a model for the dedication and sacrifice needed to both dream big, and to persevere in carrying out a big dream of writing a book, and bouncing back from the times when I thought I couldn't do it.

I also want to thank all the clergy of various denominations with whom I have watched the movies and who have heightened my own consciousness about forgiveness. Were it not for this support offered to me, both personally and by people whose professional opinions I highly respected, there would never have been the serendipity needed for Dave and me – initially a very unlikely combination – to ever meet. This book and the **P.R.I.D.E. Factor**™ are a tribute to these fortunate happenstances.

I also feel blessed and sustained by my close woman friends who are only a heartbeat away from me – my "twins": Phyllis DiAmbrosio, Ivis Villar Carey, Elizabeth Doherty, Emily Ets-Hokin, Cousin Elaine Ferguson, Margot Garfield, Alison Grabell, Judith Halbreich, La Reine Hungerford, Julie Jenczeski Moore (whom I have known since I was 3), Jane Morris, Penny Munschauer, Lisa Pearson Schwartz, Linda Pessar, Judy Ryan, Sandy Thomas, Cathy Talley Wettlauffer and the late Grace Boynton.

I want to thank my stepdaughter-in-law Nancy Rose Pearson, who first suggested that movies or videos might be helpful with Grant. Although she did not herself know about Dave's movies, she was the one who first led us in the direction of movies on big machinery. It is Geri DiCarlo whom I have to thank for selecting Grant's very first *Real Wheels* movie *There Goes a Truck* – which was our very first introduction to Dave! Who could have imagined the adventure this truck would start!

I also want to thank my personal assistant Denise Serio who tirelessly typed 20 versions of this manuscript, meticulously, conscientiously, and using her own creativity as well. I treasure her intelligence and her perceptiveness. Many times she would say to me, "Carol, honey, those last sentences that you dictated don't make sense. I can tell you were exhausted. You were really losing it. You need to go back and rewrite the end of that chapter."

I also thank editor Scott Thomas from *The Buffalo News* for his professional review of the manuscript and for his assistance in making sure my enthusiasm didn't make the manuscript become too flamboyant. I also thank my longtime friend and colleague, Father

Patrick Lynch, S.J., for his careful reading of the text, his sensitive perceptions and his editorial suggestions. I thank my friend Frances Saad for her encouragement and her goodhearted help with the references.

In addition, I want to thank my other personal assistants Aeyna Magdylan and Dale Frankosky for keeping the details of my professional and personal life in order so that I could devote myself for almost a year to this project. Otherwise I'm afraid it might have been "There Goes a Psychoanalyst's Career…"

Thanks also go to my friends chef Neal Plazio and Geri DiCarlo for keeping me fed physically while I was trying to conceptualize and write about psychological nutrition.

And lastly I want to thank the dear, loving attentiveness of my nannies, Barbara Panneri and Jacqueleine Sadd, whose empathic and loving touch sustained our whole family during the stresses of Mom's trying to complete a book in the midst of being a full-time psychoanalyst, mother and wife. Often it was unclear who needed the compassionate nannying more, Grant or me. Were I not blessed with all these connections, I could not have immersed myself in this project with Dave.

Thank you all!

# PREFACE
## A Note From Dave Hood

I am one of the luckiest people in the world. My parents and grandparents taught me that I could be anybody I wanted to be in life. I, and only I, was in control of my outcomes. They taught me a love for nature. They gave me self-confidence. The result has been a life spent doing the things that I love including radio, television, and making movies for children. Along the way I have made many mistakes but somehow I have always managed to learn from them, and move on. I have never allowed myself to be paralyzed by defeat. Somehow that message has found its way into my movies for children. Dr. Munschauer pointed out to me that as early on as 1998 before we had even consciously articulated our ideas, I said at the end of *The Adventures of Dave & Becky – In Search of Pirate Treasure Volcano* "persistence and discipline always pays off." Well, isn't that really what the **P.R.I.D.E. Factor**™ is all about: rebounding, looking forward and moving on!

I am constantly receiving e-mail from all over the world from people who love the *Dave Movies & Real Wheels* series. These usually consist of people with children who want to express thanks for the laughs and educational value the series provides for their family. Imagine my surprise when one day out of the blue a call came from "Dr. Munschauer in Buffalo, New York."

At first I wondered, was this "for real"? Was this just another enchanted "Dave" fan? Could she even be some sort of a kook? Could she really be a legitimate psychoanalyst or scholar? Dr.

Munschauer went on to explain to me that my *Real Wheels* series was not only helping her with her 4-year-old, who had a sleep disorder, but she had been actually using the tapes to *treat adult patients* in her psychoanalytic practice!

I looked into her background and discovered that she had, in fact, published quite a few articles (but never any about children's videos). She was also president of the Psychoanalytic Society of Upstate New York; and she had recently been awarded a prize from the American Psychoanalytic Society for her excellence in teaching psychoanalytic concepts to lay people. So the only question I had was, would I be able to "click" with this academic doctor? And, if she was such a "highfalutin" academic scholar, would she have a playful enough spirit in her that would enable us to work together – or even more importantly – would I be able to actually *enjoy* what might turn out to be a long-term close-up collaboration?

Many telephone calls ensued between Dr. Munschauer and myself, as we gradually got to know each other. Finally, we met in person late one night after one of my live shows in Providence, RI. She was brimming with excitement about the many subliminal positive messages she had seen in my movies (and she had become extremely immersed in all of my movies). She also was eager to tell me about the success she was having using these movies with her patients. I might add that she could hardly contain herself. I liked her enthusiasm because it reminded me, of me. There was an instant rapport and the rest is history, as they say.

The result is that the **P.R.I.D.E. Factor**™ was born. In this book Dr. Munschauer and I have tried to combine our energies and differing talents to distill a simple method that you can utilize both for yourself and for your children. With diagrams, clinical examples, and fascinating stories from real life to illustrate these techniques, we will show you how to restore success and regain happiness "even when you think you can't."

In 1990 my television show *PM Magazine* went off the air after 15 long years of success. I was out of work, the economy was at rock bottom, and I couldn't get anyone to hire me. For a person who had never been without a job since beginning his radio career at age 18, this was a devastating experience. I had no income and was virtually at the bottom looking up for the first time in my life. In a desperate attempt to find work, I moved to Hollywood where I spent the next two years being rejected by every casting director and agent I would try to see. Even my acting teachers told me that I just didn't have "it."

Finally, it occurred to me that the only way that I was going to be able to do the things that I loved, acting and directing, was if I hired myself. Why not? So I started my production company Dave Hood Entertainment, Inc. Truth be known, it existed only on paper. I didn't have any equipment or an office but what I did have was lots of experience, which I had gained over the past 20 years doing radio and television. I was able to convince a larger production company in Florida to let my company produce travel segments for its show on the Discovery Channel called *Tourific Destinations*. It was while editing one of those segments about the islands of Tahiti that the idea for *Real Wheels* was born. The series has sold more than 6 million units and in the process has influenced hundreds of thousands of children all over the world in what I hope has been a positive way.

When I first began the *Real Wheels* project I had no idea what an important part of my life it would eventually become. The thought of doing a children's show had never even entered my mind. It happened one day in 1993 at a small production house in Los Angeles when I crossed the path of a gentleman named Ken Urman and his associate Brian Levine. I was there doing some final editing on another project. Ken was in the videotape distribution business. He had little or no money for the production but what he did have was an idea for a live action children's video on how fire trucks work. He had a young child and was unhappy with what his son was watching on commercial television. It was mostly cheap animation with lots of violence disguised as humor. Somehow fate brought us together and his idea along with my experience in front of the camera and my ability to get things produced with little or no budget, gave birth to *Real Wheels*: one of the most successful and best-loved children's series in history. Kids usually refer to them as the *Dave Movies.*

Ken's idea was simple really, to show kids how fire trucks work in a live action format. My contribution was to create a real character, not animation, a character that kids would relate to. I had to make the program humorous so even 2-year-olds could enjoy it and, most importantly, to find a way to teach kids without talking down to them about all the stuff they already love: fire trucks and bulldozers. We had to do all this on a budget that any Hollywood producer would consider laughable. I thought, "Yes, I *can do* this!"

While I would like to say that each and every scene in our series was carefully written and "fully storyboarded" and researched before the actual shooting, I'm afraid that just the opposite is true. My creative team on most of the projects consisted of old friends I had worked with over the years: Scott Carter, Becky Borg, Dave Hesson and recently my wife, Rebecca. Once the subject matter was chosen, we would sit around and brainstorm about what would happen to Dave. In most cases an outline was prepared and a story line defined, but what really ended up on tape was pretty much made up as we proceeded headlong into the production not knowing exactly what we would be able to utilize on location.

I have always been one who worked from the heart. I love to ad-lib and let things just happen. I almost always try to use the first or second take because that is when the magic takes place. Just like in early live TV; unexpected moments can lead to hilarious results. In my case, I also have a real interest in machines and how they work.

I owe a great deal to my director of photography, Brad Olander, who seems to have the ability to read my mind on location while I am in front of the camera. He almost always is able to get all the shots I need. Acting as writer, director, actor and editor, the vision for the end product usually exists only in my mind. Brad somehow manages to tap into that and capture it on tape with great results.

I believe the resulting productions are a kind of Zen-influenced product. What I mean by that is that it is greatly influenced by what a person has built into his personal belief systems – those things under the surface, those things that are not written down, those things that we feel, that make up our being. These things all emerge in the final product. That's why it is so very important to be spontaneous and have fun during the shooting process, to be oneself.

The resilience and other life lessons Dr. Munschauer and I write about in this book came from that place inside. It is a place that I believe was greatly influenced by my parents and grandparents while I was growing up in a small town in Washington State. I did not purposely inject them into *Real Wheels*. They appear there because they are part of me. They are intrinsic to the way that I live my life.

I hope the **P.R.I.D.E. Factor**™ will help parents and their children rise from the ashes of defeat and conquer their worlds with pride and enthusiasm. Live every day of your life with a sparkle in your eye because you have found love for yourself and what you are doing.

*Enjoy the book!*

# CHAPTER 1

## Reviving Dreams: Introduction to The P.R.I.D.E. Factor™

Words like "success" and "greatness" are so much a part of our everyday language and vocabulary that we do not even give a second thought to what they specifically mean. We do know, almost instinctively, which children seem to be already on the "road to success," and which, as yet, have not found their way. Our language is replete with such expressions as "he's got a 'fire in his belly,'" "he's bound to become a success," "she's never lived up to her full potential," or even, "he was successful for a while, and then, for some reason, he really lost it!"

If we know success when we see it, it makes sense that we can learn how to build it – and even more importantly, how to encourage it – early on in our children. While there are literally hundreds of books that talk about techniques for self-motivation and promoting success, we know of none about how to "bounce back" after a setback or how to sustain motivation for the long run. What makes our book unique is that its focus is on how we *maintain* a feeling of success in the midst of a world, and a life, fraught with disappointments, setbacks, discouragements, and inescapable injuries and insults – experiences that often result in feelings of shame, demoralization, loss of initiative and lowered self-esteem.

Dave's and my collaboration is based on the belief that success is not a straight-line phenomenon, like a rocket lifting off at increasing speed to the moon; rather, it is a process that more resembles the ups and downs of a long-held blue chip stock in the stock market. So, part of the focus of our book is about how to raise children who are shame-resilient – who are not prone to be frequently tripping up, or collapsing, because of faults in the bedrock of their self-esteem. But our book is for adults too. Whether you are an adult or a child, the same principles apply. Our challenge, as humans, is about how to sustain, rekindle, and revitalize feelings of self-esteem and motivation after episodes of failure, injury or disappointment, and this challenge is lifelong. It is about the ability to recover and regain one's "success attitude" after the inevitable misjudgments, mishaps, missteps, and yes, even tragic catastrophes of real life. What are the necessary ingredients that go into the ability to bounce back?

Dave Hood, in his series of children's movies, was inspired on the set one day when the mantra, "Shouldn't have done that!" spontaneously came out of his mouth! This saying came from deep within his personality, without conscious intent – as is true with the creative genius of many artists – and it was this "mantra" that became the inspiration for our book. Put simply, the mantra becomes the focal point around which one has the opportunity to revitalize one's success when one has done something one "shouldn't have done." Or, to extend the meaning of the mantra: to recover when someone has done something to you that he or she "shouldn't have done." Extended even further, the opportunity and challenge begins with: How does one move on when one has been deeply affected by something that "life shouldn't have done?" These questions, and suggested answers, are the focus of our book.

This book will describe principles that are easy to learn, easy to apply, and easy to teach to both adults and children. There will be numerous examples and personal illustrations of people who have "made it," when they might not have. Our "bounce back" guidelines will be helpful to adults in their own life. We will offer understandable suggestions to help adults revive their own sense of success after times of challenge, defeat, loss, or embarrassment – be these public or private. We will also offer a model useful for raising "successful" children – that is children who have, within themselves, a capacity to "bounce back" when they need to and to go on with the story, or plot, or their own lives. This book will also be entertaining in that it will use illustrations from the movies made by Dave, as well as letting people in on some of the fascinating parts of his own personal story which led him to be able to blurt out, quite unconsciously on a movie set one day, the inspirational phrase for our book "Shouldn't have done that!"

Dave and I have distilled these messages – or principles – into what we call the **P.R.I.D.E. Factor**™ – for we believe that success is an *attitude*, not an endpoint. We will show how this *attitude* within the self can be embodied in the first letters of the five words: **P**ositivity, **R**esilience, **I**ntegrity, **D**iscipline, and **E**nthusiasm – the acronym: **P.R.I.D.E.** Maintaining the **P.R.I.D.E. Factor**™ can revitalize the self with all of the "life support systems" of the most sophisticated intensive care unit, but with none of the restrictions, constrictions, confinements, or tensions such "care units" hold. Instead, these "life support" systems are flexible, comfortable, vitalizing, enjoyable, and freeing.

**P.R.I.D.E.** is a short way of condensing the variety of attributes that go into creating the great composers in music, great masters in art, great philanthropists, great writers, and great diplomats. When we grant awards (such as the Pulitzer Prize, the Nobel Peace Prize, or *Time* magazine's Person of the Year) to these successful people, they must experience an overflowing feeling of pride after they receive the award. But this book will explain that they could never have achieved these honors had they not already had the **P.R.I.D.E. Factor**™ *first*.

As a delightful piece of personal introduction, you should know that this book is the off-spring of a very unlikely combination of partners: one, a radio personality, actor, writer, director and producer; the other (living 3,000 miles away), a mother of a 3-year-old with a sleep disorder, who is also, by career, a practicing clinical psychologist, psychoanalyst, solely academic writer and presenter.

Dave and I were living in two very different worlds and knew nothing of each other. Yet we were working on essentially the same goals: a devotion to children and to their ability to learn and absorb attitudes about success and resilience. For Dave, the focus was on how to teach children to be interested in, and to learn about and manage, intimidating machinery: dauntingly powerful monster trucks, boats, bulldozers, spaceships, fast motorcycles, race cars, transport trucks, rescue vehicles, and even military tanks. These are the sort of vehicles that little children dream about driving, but to master them takes patience, self-discipline and often the hard task of learning how to listen to instruction. Dave's movies on rescue vehicles, fire trucks, and police cars add yet another dimension: the value of learning teamwork, mutuality, and responsibility to others.

For me, the focus was on how to soothe my toddler through long periods of interrupted sleep, which caused both of us to be awakened, on and off, for long periods of time every night for 3½ years. As a psychoanalyst, I knew in my soul that in order for my son to grow up to be a resilient and successful person, he would need to learn, deep within himself, that the world was a safe place in which to be. He would need to learn that he could rely on his world to be responsive to his needs and that he could trust his caregivers. It would be this trust and confidence that would enable him enthusiastically to take on life's adventures – the very kind of adventures that Dave portrays in his movies.

As my son, Grant, and I "teamed up" together, through literally hundreds of nights of interrupted sleep, both of us had turned to various children's movies for soothing and, I hoped, for return to sleep. There were at least 40 movies in our bedside collection, but Grant kept pointing to the "Dave" movies, and I discovered that I was always personally relieved by this choice. Grant and I watched them over and over again: *There Goes a Monster Truck, There Goes a Bulldozer, There Goes a Spaceship, There Goes a Truck, There Goes a Fire Truck*, and on and on. We were both mesmerized. What had started out as painful nights for Mom (me) started to be intriguing. Dave's material began to engage my mind and to capture my attention as a psychoanalyst. "*Why* the Dave series?" I asked myself. "Why can *I* watch the Dave series over and over again, and *never* get bored? What is happening here?" And then my mind got racing (causing more sleep deprivation), and I got to thinking… and it was at that moment that Dave and I connected and this book was conceived.

With several telephone calls back and forth from East Coast to West Coast, Dave and I began to put our heads together and realized that, despite our differing models, we had both been thinking about resilience and the success attitude, or "bouncing back," but in different "languages" so to speak – Dave through entertainment, I through psychology. So we decided to meld our strengths and images together in this book. The core message is: You can revitalize a dream at any time in your journey through life, no matter what reversals you have suffered. You can "bounce back." You have the power to make it happen for yourself. With the principles Dave and I will share with you, there's not only *one* "window of opportunity," or only *one* "developmental phase" when growth and success are possible (as some older psychological theories once taught us). Rather, change and growth are possible *throughout* life.

If you think of yourself as a flower, it is true, sometimes a weed presses on you – sometimes it can be a very big weed, indeed. Sometimes big feet step on you. Sometimes you even get chopped up a bit in a lawnmower. But, as you will see from this book, you are never powerless. Even if stones and rubble are thrown upon you in the form of shame, defeat, fear and anxiety, you must remember that the flower always "wants" to grow. It is the flower's nature to "want" to succeed and develop. The trick is merely to decide to help that flower and to provide it with the full nourishment it needs. The drive for success and vitality that is within *us all* can then be allowed to blossom and flourish again.

Now, sometimes the rocks, the dirt, and rubble, so to speak, have been there for a *very, very* long time, snuffing out the bloom of the flower. But Dave and I are firm believers in personal archaeology. A nascent, budding flower, ready for tending, can be uncovered in *all* of us. When the "nutrients" needed for growth can be provided, the innate beauty and success potential in any living being can be enabled to shine through. "So come what may – tempest, drought, old age, illness – we can remain green, viable and growing with hope and love." (John J. McNeill, p.155)

For adults, digging out from under the debris that has accumulated through years of living is what this book is about. For parents, learning when and where to avoid shoveling rubble on your developing child is what this book is about. It is as simple a concept as that... to learn not to get in the way of the flower's innate program of blooming and developing.

I was once treating a 93-year-old patient who had been in analysis with me (and still blossoming, I might add) for 10 years. I marveled to her: "Do you know how fortunate you are? You have three wonderfully successful children: *all* successful professionally, *all* good human beings, and they all love each other. And to add to that, all your successful children have professionally successful grandchildren who all love each other. And, furthermore, the *whole lot* of them *love you*! You have really done a wonderful job raising them." She looked at me very seriously and quizzically, and replied, "I didn't raise them." Taken aback I responded, "What do you mean, you didn't raise them? You were home full time; you had no nannies or help or day care; you didn't work; of course you raised them!"

7

Still looking at me, rather blankly and soberly she said, "I didn't raise them: all I did was find out who they were." What a perfect description of allowing a flower to become all that it can be!

Likewise, a man I know had a child who chose to live an alternative lifestyle. Some friends of this man, knowing that the lifestyle his child chose was in conflict with some of his strongly held values, asked him, "How are you doing with your son's choices? Are you very upset?" The man, wise beyond his years, responded, "What is it for me to be upset? I just love watching the metamorphosis of all my children as they grow."

Watching the multiple illustrations of "bouncing back" and resilience in the Dave movies, and the way that the characters allow each other to be who they are without shaming or devaluing each other, intrigued me and made me want to find out what sort of unique factors had been present in Dave's own childhood development that had provided him with such a natural intuition about resilience. In fact, the "success attitude" is so interwoven throughout Dave's movies that I fully expected to find it to be an integral part of his own personal life and a deep part of his psyche. So, when I learned that Dave's mother had been influenced by the ideas in the Rev. Norman Vincent Peale's book *The Power of Positive Thinking*, I felt affirmed! Perhaps this is one of the basic reasons that Dave absorbed, so early on, the natural aptitude for "bouncing back."

Not all people have had as propitious beginnings as Dave has, with his mother's deep investment in the positivity messages of Norman Vincent Peale (and the input of his easy-going, nonjudgmental father, whom we will tell you more about later). But, both Dave and I share the belief that despite one's background, one can kindle, or rekindle, one's own "pilot light" and move forward again. To emphasize what I have said before, what first caught my attention about Dave's movies was how the "Dave character" never got *stuck* in anger, despair, or vengeance, despite whatever setbacks, mishaps, or even potentially shaming incidents he encountered in his own various journeys and adventures. And, as I got to know the *real* Dave, I found that was the essence, not only of his wonderful series of uplifting children's movies, but also of the way he thinks about, and lives, his own life. *never got stuck in anger, despair or vengeance.*

I discovered that Dave consciously began many years ago to focus on formulating his ideas about how one maintains enthusiasm and goal-directedness in the face of life's ups and downs. He also told me that he writes letters to himself and keeps journals about how people can maintain a sense of vitality or aliveness. So, we joyfully discovered our common interest and decided to collaborate on this book, dedicated to helping people learn about what factors contribute to the development of children's "success attitude." The book also gives guidance about what adults can do to maintain or regain their own sense of vitality, regardless of the particular circumstances of their own childhoods.

Here is an example:

A terrible fire consumed the home of a family I know. Some friends returned with the children to the scene of the fire that same afternoon, and waited while the children, still in shock and disbelief, sifted through the ashes. It turned

9

out that only two things could be found in the remains: some articles of smoke-damaged clothing and their intact basketball. The children insisted on dusting off and retrieving their ball, and their friend, attuned to the significance of their having unearthed that ball, took the children to a nearby playground, where they played a basketball game with that very ball. He then helped the children find a bell jar in which to encase the ball. Although no words were exchanged, the friend had intuitively helped the children assemble this bell jar because he knew that the children had recognized, however inchoately, that this ball had become the symbol of their own survival... their own resilience and potential usefulness... and their own ability to survive and to "bounce back."

(Courtesy of Aeyna Magdylen)


In short, one gets on with life by accepting oneself and valuing the life that is still to come. As a friend and colleague of mine, Dominican Father Sam Mattarazzo, has said, "It is faith in the future that brings life."

For Sigmund Freud "the ability to love and to work" was the key to mental health. Dave and I would add that it is the ability to *recover* the capacity to love and to work after loss, injury, or disappointment that is the true marker of a successful life.

Interestingly enough, while on the surface, Dave in his movies was teaching children about how things *worked*, in the subtext he was really communicating about *love*: love of one's self and love of other people. He was teaching about resilience and about forgiveness. Likewise, while on the surface, I was trying to be a *loving* mother, to soothe my child through distressingly sleepless nights and build a bedrock of security, I found my mind *working* overtime (as an increasingly sleep-deprived psychoanalyst), trying to put into words the deep lessons about resilience and personal success that I was watching in Dave's movies.

So, in a nutshell, Freud would be pleased. This book is a blend of love and work. It will hopefully offer enlightenment and guidance about how to raise healthy, resilient, enthusiastic and successful children and give inspiration to adults during life's road of ups and downs. We hope that in reading it you will both have fun and discover that the process of "bouncing back" and holding on to the "success attitude" is not as complicated as it may seem. By the time you have read this book and absorbed the principles behind the **P.R.I.D.E. Factor**™, your grasp on its essentials should be almost intuitive. That's why we call this book our "Little Text for Big Success."

**CHAPTER 2**

## Resilience & Hope

Since some of the recent large-scale tragedies, including the downing of the twin towers in New York City, there has been a surge of interest among psychologists in resilience, grief, recovery, post-traumatic stress disorder (PTSD) and delayed post-traumatic stress disorder. In a recent article entitled "Loss, Trauma, and Human Resilience," psychologist George Bonanno says that "studies estimate that the majority of the U.S. population has been exposed to at least one traumatic event, defined using *DSM-III* criteria of an event outside the range of normal human experience, during the course of their lives." (*American Psychologist*, January 2004) He continues on to say that "as developmental psychologists have long asserted, there is no single means of maintaining equilibrium following highly aversive events, but rather there are multiple and sometimes unexpected pathways to resilience." The point of his article, which reviews much of the current literature, is that the field of psychology has greatly underestimated the innate capacity of resilience in most of us even after extraordinarily disruptive and stressful events.

Dave's movie *There Goes a Bulldozer* opens with a dramatic visual image: a series of imposing structures – sequentially all blowing up: a building, a dike, a bridge. We see them crumbling into fragments; then, in seconds, they resurrect and restore themselves again before our very eyes. We are amused as we watch this over and over again, building after building. A feeling of awe and incredulity overtakes us – concrete structures larger than life, yet structures that can be used as metaphors for our own lives. Dave and I share the conviction that the *success attitude* is not about how often one falters, flops, fails, or falls, but *how often one gets up again.*

Our book is about personal success and *resilience*. To paraphrase the psychologist Masten (2001): resilience is defined as good outcomes which prevail in spite of serious threats to adaptation or development. Dave's movies illustrate this definition very clearly because they are dramatic stories which show that a successful outcome almost always has its ups and downs. Whether we are studying stories of success in real life or watching movies such as Dave's, one is continually reminded that success is rarely a linear phenomenon. One does not just "set out" to become successful and continue on without interruption. Because of this message, Dave's movies hold a tremendous attraction for children and adults alike. In his movies, Dave refreshingly illustrates examples of how individuals and relationships can maintain their cohesion and pull themselves back together after failure, disappointment or defeat.

The fragmentation of concrete in *There Goes a Bulldozer* is symbolic of our sense of ourselves. We are all subject to fluctuating states of wellbeing from day to day. Understanding what is happening as we go through these fluctuating states is extremely helpful.

For example, if you watch yourself carefully, it is normal to observe feelings of going "up and down" emotionally at various times during the day, depending on things that happen – even small things. Our self-esteem can oscillate from day-to-day, hour-to-hour and sometimes even minute-to-minute, depending on who or what comes our way. Our sense of vitality, our sense of openness and confidence, our sense of feeling more withdrawn, insecure, or strange varies according to what "hits us" in our environment. Psychologists call these differing or shifting "self-states." Our "concrete," so to speak, wiggles and jiggles. Sometimes it crumbles, and sometimes it even falls to pieces. The trick is to somehow be able to bring it back together again – not quite in the way Dave can, by just rewinding the tape and making the bridge resurrect, but somehow we *need* to bring ourselves back into a state of cohesion. And this is the focus of our book.

More needs to be said about "concrete." Some causes of these jiggles and wiggles, these jars to our self-esteem, are everyday matters: A friend doesn't greet us when we pass on the street; someone who says that he'll call us doesn't call; we have a party and expected guests do not come; a publisher doesn't accept one of our treasured manuscripts; someone we look up to in the world falls short of our expectations. These are everyday occurrences. It is normal to feel destabilized by these things. It is normal to feel shaken up.

Some of us can more easily pull ourselves together, straighten up, and move forward. We have more of what psychologists have long ago termed the personality trait of hardiness (Kobasa, Maddi, and Kahn, 1982) to buffer us against extreme stress.

"Hardiness consists of three dimensions, being committed

to finding meaningful purpose in life, the belief that one can influence one's surroundings and the outcome of events and the belief that one can learn and grow from both positive and negative life experiences." (Bonnano, 2004, p. 25)

Others, who are not so hardy, remain in fragments for a long time, or resort to self-defeating behaviors to try to pull together again – such as alcoholism, sex, drug abuse, or rage reactions. The point is that no one of us is completely immune from disagreeable disruptions. Some people are more prone to having these disruptions more easily or more severely or for a longer period of time because their underlying self-esteem is more fragile. Their budding flower, so to speak, has not received the kind of nourishment that should have been provided by its environment and so it has been left more vulnerable.

The good news Dave and I wish to impart is that past history does not have to determine one's fate. In Chapter 5, we will discuss more about how people, even if they have had injuries or deprivations during their childhoods that have left them more vulnerable, can be active in strengthening themselves when a crisis has beset them. Even though you may feel stuck, you are not fated to stay stuck. For, to quote Marcel Proust:

"The real voyage of discovery consists not in seeing new landscapes,
but in having new eyes."

In no way do we mean to minimize the intensity of the pain

of a setback in one's life. When one suffers a reversal, or injury, a natural feeling of helplessness can occur no matter what one's background has been. Those who have had more interpersonal support in their childhood can be more at an advantage, because they might have learned some helpful skills early on about how and where to turn to fortify themselves. But for those who have not had such advantageous beginnings, it is never too late to learn these skills and bounce back (and to teach them to your children). Much more will be said about this idea in Chapter 5.

What do we mean when we talk about a crisis? In this book, a crisis is defined as one of three situations: One, "I shouldn't have done that!" (something that you have done that is clearly a mistake, an error, or something to regret); two, "you shouldn't have done that!" (something that has been done to you that was unwanted, or resented); and three, "life shouldn't have done that to me!" (a life event such as a financial reversal, a reverse in one's physical health, job, or personal relationship, that has caused hurt or personal setback).

These "shouldn't have" experiences, as crises, are, by definition, turning points. And, psychologists have long held that, as with all turning points, crises, if handled well, can often rapidly move things forward for the better. Crises, if *not* handled well, can often lead to greater grief. If you look back over the crises in your own life, or the lives of others you know, it is likely that all of them fall into one of these three "shouldn't have" categories.

A *Montel* show, aired in August 2003, featured guests who experienced unrelenting feelings of guilt for what they "shouldn't have done," such as a parent who mistakenly ran over his child, killing her, and a father who, by accident, shot his son while handling his gun.

The newspapers are replete with stories of people who "shouldn't have done that," and then commit suicide when sexual impropriety, financial mismanagement or some other misdeed is publicly revealed. Many acts of revenge, hate crimes and chronic attitudes of intolerance happen because of the conviction that "you shouldn't have done that." Recently Father John Geoghan, a priest convicted of child molestation, was murdered in a maximum-security prison by a neo-Nazi prisoner who himself had been molested as a child. And, the conflict in the Middle East reflects centuries of grievances and revenge for what people "shouldn't have done" to each other.

And, there are many cases of "life shouldn't have done that," where people either retreat into despair or depression, or, on the other hand, are able to regroup, reintegrate, remobilize, and find somewhere within themselves the resilience to invent a new life – often to their own surprise. Christopher Reeve was a model of someone who bounced back and found a new life making strides in science for people who are paralyzed; actor David Lander, who played Squiggy on the old television sitcom *Laverne and Shirley*, has devoted his life to educating people about multiple sclerosis.

When there has been a "shouldn't have done that," one individual commits suicide or murder, becomes a substance abuser, or is perpetually stuck in guilt, depression and shame; another individual transforms his life, elevates and motivates the lives of other people, and is able to make new dreams come true. What is the difference among these people?

For example, I know of a painter whose work was known for its delicacy of line and texture. One day he had a stroke and was unable to fully use one side of his body. However, instead of succumbing to despair, he began to paint standing up, using his whole torso, in (atypical for him) large, muscular body movements. The whole tenor of his creative expression changed. Suddenly his work drew the attention of art critics, his work became widely known and he was making a small fortune in sales.

By contrast, I have a patient whose father died when the patient was 6 years old, and her mother went into a total collapse. Her mother wore black every day for the rest of her life (which was 40 years), refused to socialize or leave the house, drank heavily, and held on to the belief that this behavior was an extended visible signature of grief and a sign of loyalty to her prematurely lost husband. The shadow of darkness cast over the rest of the family by this victimhood sapped the vitality, spirit and sense of independence for the next two generations that followed. Not until one young member of the family went into analysis was the intergenerational family myth that despair represents a familial pledge of allegiance – was this spell broken, and younger members of the family were released to experience joy.

The inescapable truth is that life is such that none of us is immune from having to deal with some sort of defeat or serious challenge. No one is granted immunity from the unexpected and unwelcomed happenstances of "bad things happening to good people" (Kushner), the slings and arrows of natural or unnatural forces, or defeats due to other people's conflicting interests. Our troubles can range from misstarts and misadventures, to horrible tragedies and unspeakable losses, and a whole range of painful experiences in-between.

In *The Road Less Traveled*, M. Scott Peck's first sentence is "Life is difficult." Even the message of the biblical prophets was that we are all going to have trouble in the world. The problem is not whether we have trouble, but how we deal with it, how we overcome it, and how not to be overcome by it. This book is about what can be learned to enable people to either not collapse after a "shouldn't have done that" experience, or to not have to *stay* collapsed for very long. The goal is always to be able to bounce back and to move forward. Author Robert Louis Stevenson is inspirational in this regard when he said, "Life is not just holding good cards, but being able to play the bad ones as well."

Dave himself was always undeterred by "ups and downs." He learned about success by focusing his energy on a goal, going full-steam towards it. But if he made an error, he admitted his mistake, corrected it, geared up and went at it full steam again. In *In Search of Pirate Treasure Volcano*, after returning home and finally successfully finding the golden treasure, Dave announces his maxim to the viewer: "Persistence and discipline always pays."

Dave's own mother told me, "I believe Dave went into the world knowing that the thoughts he thinks, the decisions he makes and the actions he takes control his destiny – thus he is happy with life and simply bounces back if something doesn't go smoothly, and continues on." In fact, it is Dave's own philosophy that many high achievers actually profit from failing (or, in his movies, falling), because it gives them a new perspective that they might not have considered before, and fresh opportunities to do things differently. For example, in *There Goes a Race Car*, viewers learn that it is OK to ask for help. The ability to solicit human assistance if one is lost or stuck is indeed an important life skill to learn. So Dave agrees with Cicely Tyson that "Challenges make you discover things about yourself that you never really knew. They're what makes the instrument stretch – what makes you go beyond the norm."

The theme of not being afraid to try new things, even if it means failure, is seen vividly in the Dave movies, where many (often many, many) mishaps occur and Dave has to pull himself together and continue on. He would agree with publisher Malcom S. Forbes that "Failure is success if we learn from it." In one movie dream sequence, Dave is literally flattened by the roller on the front of a bulldozer, and he has to get up, dust himself off, and take on an easier task more suited to his abilities. He falls down a hill in *There Goes a Rescue Truck* and has to regroup; he gets snared by a hook at a construction site in *There Goes a Truck*; he falls into the back of a garbage truck in *There Goes a Garbage Truck*; and he even takes a tumble down a cliff in *There Goes a Spaceship*. In all of these scenarios, he has to restore himself and, more importantly, his self-esteem and move forward – he has to "bounce back." Dave literally makes true the maxim, "Fall seven times, stand up eight." (Janice Powers)

As an amusing aside, here I would like to add that Dave's sister, Pat Hood (who is 2½ years younger), shared with me a family anecdote that, when I told Dave about it, he did not even remember!

To a psychoanalyst's mind, both the anecdote itself, as well as his not remembering it as anything unusual, indicate how ingrained this particular theme is in the makeup of Dave's personality.

When Dave was a boy, he would torment his younger sister by pretending, very dramatically (as only Dave can do), that he was having a massive heart attack. He would clutch his chest, make choking sounds, bump against the walls, and drop precipitously onto the kitchen floor feigning a sudden death. When his sister responded with shock and fear, that the most horrible, irreversible, unthinkable event had happened (her admired older brother had "croaked"), Dave would bounce back up again, victorious, vivacious and giggling. Apparently he repeated this trick over and over throughout their youth. And to Dave's glee and his sister's dismay, this practical joke worked on his sister many, many times!

Hearing this story made it clear to me that Dave was mastering the concept of loss and reconstruction, even as a youngster. And now these very themes are the center of Dave's movies and the subject of this book. (And now, thanks to the adventures of modern science, many people today are blessed to be able to bounce back from serious heart attacks!) Dave's sister explained further, "I've always observed that Dave found a way to learn from disappointments, to learn to turn those experiences into lessons that made him stronger." And it is easy to see how this dynamic has influenced Dave's work.

While the fragments of a concrete bridge cannot zoom back together and physically become the same structure again in real life, the message of comfort portrayed in the Dave series is that cohesion can be restored after injury. Metaphorically, our pieces can come back together. The spiritually healing message we get from Dave is that when a person's sense of self-esteem feels shattered, or a relationship is injured, or even badly disrupted, there does not have to be condemnation of the self or of another. What a wonderful message to give to our children and to ourselves!

In the midst of entertaining stories, the Dave movies offer a message of healing and hope in this subcontext. These are the messages that seep into our hearts and souls. No matter what goes wrong, or who disappoints whom, there is no lasting contempt, rejection, or unhealable resentment; that is, there is no "deal breaker." Life's adventures and explorations, and all the antics continue on. The saga is not derailed by the crisis. And this is because everyone's self-esteem is maintained.

Let's define "self-esteem," since it is a word that is bandied about often. Psychologist Nathaniel Branden defines it as "the disposition to experience one's self as being competent to cope with the basic challenges of life and being worthy of happiness." So, what is striking in the Dave movies is that despite disappointments and even traumatic letdowns (like the truck running out of gas because Dave didn't check the fuel gauge, or there's no food for the picnic on the motorcycle trip because Becky dropped the picnic basket), there is never any shaming of the self or shaming of the other. What a relief! How unusual in our day and age! *People long for these messages*! How different our world would be if this were the tenor of our lives.

One of the examples that strikes me most in this regard is an advertisement that runs on television around Christmastime every year put on by the Seventh Day Adventists. I will only paraphrase it because I do not have the exact lines. A little boy comes running in to his house filled with exuberance and feelings of pride. He calls out to some parent figure with great glee describing all of the subjects in which he received A's and B's and all of the wonderful awards he had just gotten at the end of the semester. You could see the glow in this little child by both his body movements and the expression on his face. The screen door slams behind him and all you hear is a reprimanding voice from the top of the stairs yelling out at him in reproach "How many times have we told you not to slam the screen door?!" Viewers can palpably feel the wound to the little boy's heart as his enthusiasm is abruptly dashed. One small fragment of his entire presentation is singled out and found to be flawed, and shame overshadows what could have been a proud and joyful moment for him and for the whole family. How dreadfully sad.

Dave's movies also set themselves apart from other popular children's cartoons and videos where revenge themes abound: Animals chase each other around and "Bam! Bam! Bam!" each other on the head. Pictures of seeing stars illustrate the magnitude of the blow, often to the point of unconsciousness. Characters cause each other to be knocked off cliffs, or get squished by a boulder in response to some real or perceived injury. Cops and robbers shoot at each other around corners of buildings in order to establish dominance or to take revenge when "someone done me wrong." And even when the retaliation is not physical, children are exposed over and over to a type of ping-pong game of injury and shame. One character feels put down, and responds by shaming or ridiculing the other, and then the first responds in kind, but by upping the ante.

In the age in which we live, when grudges and anger can burn forever, when people seek revenge or never forgive, when people can't forgive themselves, Dave is a refreshing role model. He offers hope that disappointments can be managed, and that adversity, whether it be due to poor judgment, awkwardness, klutziness or other behavioral imperfections (such as not listening to the instructor), can be overcome and that a happy, good life can ensue. He quotes Victoria Holt:

"Never regret. If it's good, it's wonderful, if it's bad, it's experience."

In fact, the refreshing message of no terminal damnation of the self, or the other, has drawn in millions of viewers of the Dave movies and attracted Dave to Public Broadcasting Stations across the country. This message of forward-looking hope – hope for life and hope for survival (certainly the ultimate form of success in some cases) – must account not only why so many children facing terminal cancer ask to meet Dave through the Make-A-Wish Foundation, but also why 7,000 fans appeared at Dave's live show in Denver's Pepsi Center just four days after the Sept. 11, 2001, attack on the World Trade Center (the day some refer to as "America's darkest day"). Most performances were cancelled that week. The airlines were not flying. But Dave drove the 22 hours from San Diego to Denver to not disappoint the kids. Dave's belief in resilience resonates with American historian Charles Beard's comment "When it is dark enough, you can see the stars."

To summarize, for Dave, a successful life is not defined as one free of setbacks, or disappointment, or pain, but it is one of recognizing these emotions, recognizing one's responsibility (or lack of it) for these emotions, and continuing to grow beyond the negative event toward positive outcomes – toward making big dreams come true. He believed in Albert Einstein's philosophy "In the middle of difficulty lies opportunity."

Blessed by the influence of his mother's thinking, Dave had, from very early on, internalized deep within his nature an inclination to look at the bright side. So, we can say that Dave had, indeed, a fortunate head start.

It is a stunning fact that 10 years ago there were about 100 psychological studies on sadness for every one study on happiness. Now, however, there is a burgeoning "positive psychology" movement, which is spearheaded by University of Pennsylvania psychologist Martin Seligman. This movement devotes itself to teaching people about optimism, mastery of negative experiences and emotions, and how to employ what psychoanalyst George Valliant (2000) calls "adaptive coping strategies."

It is exciting for me as a psychoanalyst to discover how Dave's work is resonating with the contemporary focus of positive psychology and the refreshing message that human beings possess the potential to restore themselves and "bounce back" if they are willing to take proactive steps. Whether there is loss, disgrace, rejection, ridicule, or any other "shouldn't have done that" experience, a ball that can still bounce can be retrieved from the ashes (as in the example of the fire in Chapter 1) and the next chapter of life can begin! This attitude of future potential and moving on is crucial for both individuals and for our society. As a matter of fact, the American Psychological Association has devoted this year to a campaign about teaching resilience, and psychologist George Bonanno in an article in the January 2004 *American Psychologist* urges, "As we move into the next millennium it will be imperative to take a fresh look at the various ways people adapt and even flourish in the face of what otherwise would seem to be potentially debilitating events." (p. 20)

As with that ball encased in the bell jar, this book will give you ideas, guidelines, and direction to remind you of your hope and to teach you how to "bounce back." As NFL football coach Mike Ditka said, "Success isn't permanent and failure isn't fatal."

## CHAPTER 3

## "I SHOULDN'T HAVE DONE THAT!"
## THE KEY TO MOVING FORWARD...

In this chapter we will take a closer look at the charisma that drew Dave and me together. This was our shared knowledge that success is not a goal or endpoint, but rather an *attitude*. For anyone who has watched the movies, Dave's mantra " I shouldn't have done that!" is the main attraction. The allure of those words seems to seep into our pores like a healing salve. This is because it connects with some of our deepest wounds, anxious regrets, and often hidden shame reactions that are so much of our shared, everyday human drama. The goal of this chapter is to deepen the wisdom behind this mantra.

During my sleepless nights, my attention increasingly became riveted on that phrase: "I shouldn't have done that!" And it was not just the phrase that captivated me. It was the whole sequence of events that either happened, or more importantly *did not happen*, after the behavior that "shouldn't have been done" occurred. This whole process – an event ("I shouldn't have done that!," or "you shouldn't have done that," or "life shouldn't have done that"), then a sequel of *pleasant* and interesting activities and adventures, soaked into my exhausted self like a healing emollient. It occurred to me that Dave was capturing the essence of a calming message that all people, young and old, are in search of, a type of psychic "holy grail." The combination of the injury (the "I shouldn't have done that"), the restoration of the injury, and the later progression to *good* events and happy outcomes, along with a healing of the injury and freedom from guilt and shame is the freeing message embedded in all of Dave's stories. It is this message, I believe, that brings people to watch his works over and over (now more than $50 million in retail sales).

The character, Dave, seems *always* to be running into glitches. There are all sorts of tasks that he's trying to master. At times he is ridiculously clumsy. He seems to flub up constantly. There are friends he disappoints and friends he fails. But somehow, it is never a terrible calamity. It's never condemnatory. It's never unforgivable. Dave shows that people can be imperfect; they can be klutzy. They can have problems, really "blow it," and still continue to believe in themselves. They can still maintain a "success attitude," and proceed on with life's adventures. They can master difficult tasks, learn to drive huge vehicles, and even if they really goof up or behave "disastrously" along the way, their pride and self-esteem can be kept intact. Bad things can happen, even very bad things, but as we explained in the last chapter, resilience is about changing your way of looking at events and your way of responding to the events that have happened. As journalist Anna Quindlen urges, "Call it a correction, not a crisis."

In fact, the Dave character in the movies attracts us because he is a guy with whom everyone can identify. It is this common humanity that is the appeal. All of us have had experiences where we have actually failed, or just imagined that we have failed. Maybe we sense that others think that we have failed. Often, it is the accumulation of these gnawing aches of shame and regret that can overcome us, or make us stumble. All of us can identify with the pangs of anxiety, anger, and hurt that accumulate just by living life, by trying things and failing – failing ourselves, or failing others. Such injuries can cause ill feelings between loved ones and rough edges between friends. They can make us physically ill, or even precipitate wars. Witness the hostilities in the Middle East, which have been going on since before the birth of Christ.

Dave gives a model of someone who is able to disappoint, or be disappointed, and everyone he interacts with *stays* "*OK.*" Calamities, near catastrophe, and all sorts of situational "pickles" all eventually work out. No incident becomes a "deal breaker." There are a lot of tense moments. There are a lot of embarrassing happenstances. But the mantra "I shouldn't have done that!" overrides the shame and the adventure proceeds. The message is that people do make mistakes, and, more importantly, that people can *admit* that they make mistakes and move on.

The key is that the message "I made a mistake" can be separated from "I *am* a mistake." "What I *do*" can be differentiated from "Who I *am*." Dave can separate out "I *did* something dumb" from "I *am* dumb." He can separate out "I failed at this" from "I *am* a failure." As one patient of mine put it, "I need to learn to see the difference between 'I *had* an emotional dip,' from 'I *am* a dip.'"

The message we need to transmit to our children is that what they *do* may not always be good, but who they *are* is good. And they need to hear this over and over again, because they do not naturally think this way. An example is my now 4-year-old son:

29

One day he came home from school and was crying, repeatedly telling me how "bad" he had been. I inquired what he meant, since he is a loving, gentle child and I could not imagine his being "bad" in school – yet he insisted that he was bad and was crying and quite inconsolable. He told me that he had hit another child. He told me how angry he had been that the child had taken away one of his playthings and that he had hit him because of it.

We had a long discussion about how hurt he must have been that his toy had been taken from him, but how hitting is not good. I explained to Grant that he could have gone to the teacher and asked for another toy or gone to find another toy to play with on his own. After school hours, I called the teacher to ask what in the world had happened that day! She was shocked and surprised to hear his story and told me that no hitting had occurred at all that day! She said that she had been close to my son all day long and that he had behaved extremely well.

As I took the time to "debrief" my son further, he revealed to me that he had had the desire to hit the other child, but had not *really* hit him. Then I realized that he could not, as yet, differentiate his thoughts from his actions. In his own little mind, they were the same. Because he had *wanted* to hit the other child who had taken his toy, for my son, it was the same as having actually hit him. (Remember

President Jimmy Carter's confession of having lusted over hundreds of women!)

I spent a long time trying to help Grant understand the difference between wanting to hit someone, and actually hitting him or her. I tried to emphasize that his behavior was really very "good," because we can have "bad thoughts" and still behave well. But I realize that I will have to have this same discussion with him many, many, many more times.

Sometimes, even adults do not outgrow the feeling that the thought and the deed are the same thing. They equate having thought something bad with actually "being" bad. This is especially true if their parents have not taken the time to help them differentiate what they *do* from who they *are*. Dave's constant emphasis, subtle as it is portrayed in his movies, is a wonderful antidote for children who might be facing the potential of later condemning themselves for their natural thoughts and feelings. In his movies Dave never says he *is* bad. Also, he never ever characterizes people who disappoint him as bad. Despite hurt, disappointment and injury, the response is always "shouldn't have done that!" with a focus on the behavior without comment about the intrinsic value of the person.

What also makes the Dave stories unique is that Dave, in all his movies, remains so identifiably human. Most media characters are portrayed as either perfect, ideal heroes, or "hardship cases." Often they are previously idealized people, prior supermen, who later get caught doing something horrendous, such as murdering someone, betraying their company or their stockholders, or making dangerous drug deals. The Dave character is unique in that he always portrays an everyday, common guy in understandable predicaments that the viewer can picture himself suffering. Frequently he can be seen as a childlike figure who has grandiose ideas and expectations of himself, but when he fails, the refreshing part is that he is not devastated, defeated or destroyed – either within his own heart, or by others around him. Often he is able to use his fantasy life in a healthy way to *play with* ideas of superiority in order to rekindle his own motivation and re-ignite his sense of vitality. (For example, when he finds himself mortified on his own motorcycle, stranded with no gas and no food in the middle of a rainstorm, he goes under a tree, looks up into the sky and fantasizes a stunning motorcycle race where he wins a big trophy and gets a big kiss from a beautiful blonde!)

Modern biologists, such as Waddington (1996) use the term "self-righting" to describe the capacity to recover from disruptions and restore motivation. This concept is similar to traction control systems (TCS) in automobiles that redirect a car if it's skidding (DiAmbrosio 2005). Individuals who are resilient are able to "steer the course" even when events intervene, either from within themselves, or externally from the environment. This "self-righting" can be done through fantasy (as Dave does in fantasizing about winning the motorcycle race) or through actually coping differently with things in one's environment. Beethoven, for example, was able to transcend, or self-right, from his depression about his hearing loss by writing his Ninth Symphony. Though aware of his growing deafness, he was not overcome by it but was able to move on with his joyful creation, still conscious of his pain as he composed the piece (Forbes, 1969).

In her 1996 book *The Transcendent Child: Tales of Triumph over the Past*, author Lillian Rubin reports on children who are not rendered helpless by an event but who can transcend it. One way they transcend events is by healthy, constructive, restorative use of fantasy. The ability to fantasize is important for children and for adults. When a woman has a miscarriage, she often fantasizes immediately about another pregnancy. Often, when people divorce, they fantasize about having another kind of relationship. And Dave constantly reminds people that all sorts of big fantasies are doable. A typical ending to one of his movies is: "with learning, and staying in school, *you* too can be a monster truck driver!" He reminds us, over and over again, not to give up on our fantasies – no matter how out of reach they may seem, and he exemplifies what psychologist Christopher Peterson has called the "Big Optimism" – the belief that a person will be able to survive regardless of life's circumstances. It is as if the words of Helen Keller have resonated both through his personal life and also through his artistic work, "No pessimist ever discovered the secrets of the stars, or sailed to an uncharted land, or opened a new heaven to the human spirit."

Dave had fantasies in real life. When he was young, he pictured himself being very popular, even hosting a national television show. He could gain enthusiasm, comfort and pride from picturing himself on radio and television. It was a fantasy that lifted his spirits, because he knew in his heart that he was destined for success. Later his fantasy did come true. Dave has tapes of his radio shows and his television adventures from all over the world during his many years hosting and producing the show *PM Magazine_*and_*Tourific Destinations* on the Discovery Channel. Sometimes, as Dave's movies show, children's fantasies (even if they are first used to make us feel better) do come true.

And speaking of fantasies, the theme that first began to lure me to Dave's movies in the middle of those sleepless nights was the "wonderland" Dave's stories created where the characters never devalued each other or put each other down. No matter what happened, no matter what glitch or disappointment came up – no matter whose car was driven over or whose bridge was blown up, there was no name-calling, no shaming, no unending grudges, just "shouldn't have done that!" Whether we were looking at trucks, or bulldozers, or spaceships, or motorcycle racetracks, this was indeed wondrous! Dave portrays relational experiences that are respectful, enhancing, supportive and able to contain emotionally intense feelings – what a wonderful model for children and adults alike. "How is Dave making Grant and me feel so good?" I asked myself from my happy, fantastical state.

The way Dave moves through his difficulties is a three-step process. First, he *owns* his mistake. He admits the deed about which he feels shame with the very simple mantra, "I shouldn't have done that!" Second, he is willing to learn from his mistake, and to have an open mind about being instructed and corrected. Third, he maintains an attitude that permits him to move forward without holding a grudge against himself or anyone else. So, with these three simple steps, Dave portrays a model for forgiveness of self, forgiveness of the other, and shame resilience.

More thoughts about shame are in order here. Shame and guilt are often confused, but they differ significantly. While guilt is a feeling that one has *done* something wrong, shame is a feeling that there *is* something wrong or defective with one's *self*. It is the feeling of defectiveness, or of not being "good enough" in some important way. Psychoanalyst Andrew Morrison describes the "language of shame." By this he means that feelings of shame are often disguised in everyday words such as "foolish," "weak," "silly," "dumb," "lazy," "inadequate," "worthless," "helpless," and "stupid." Whenever we hear these words expressed, it is an indication that the person saying them is really feeling the emotion of shame.

People want to talk about guilt and can even feel internally pressed to talk about it, because their experience has been, or they have learned, that if they confess their guilt, they will be forgiven, or they can atone. There are even religious rituals that provide for this process in a formal way. On the other hand, feelings of shame usually are hidden and not talked about. Not only are they hidden, but they are also extraordinarily painful to reveal. I have heard many patients describe their feelings of shame as "searingly" painful. It is natural then that they would want to hide these feelings both from themselves, and certainly, from other people.

Another bothersome aspect of shame feelings is that they are frequently contagious. When a person describes his feelings of shame, it often reminds the listener of his own feelings of shame which may have been, at least at that point, out of awareness. So shame can spread like a nasty fungus, making the atmosphere unhealthy all around.

Shaming another person is one of the most effective ways our culture has to control behaviors (and in some other cultures, it is appallingly even more so). A common example is road rage. When we cut someone off on the road, his automatic reaction is to feel personally diminished and unimportant, as if "you don't care about me," or "you don't honor my space or my welfare." So, he makes an angry finger gesture to reciprocate and diminish the self-esteem of the driver who cut him off. The first driver, feeling dually diminished, typically returns the gesture, and then the gesture is returned again. It's a type of shaming ping-pong match that regrettably all too often escalates into dangerous confrontation. Lauren Slater said in a February 2003 *New York Times* article, "In 1990, David Long published *The Anatomy of Terrorism*, in which he found that hijackers and suicide bombers suffer from feelings of worthlessness and that their violent, fluorescent acts are desperate attempts to bring some inner flair to a flat mindscape." We get a vivid sense from this quote about the desperate and dramatic efforts people will effect in order to counter what can be seen as basic underlying feelings of weakness and worthlessness – shame feelings.

With these insights in mind, how bizarre it seems that advertisers, on an everyday basis, choose to evoke shame for the purpose of selling products. "You smell bad"; "you're too fat"; "your cellulite is showing"; "you must get rid of those wrinkles." Teachers use shame to control students: "You're a failure"; you wear a "dunce" cap; you're given detention; "you're a flunky"; "you're a brat!" Parents use shame to control their children: "You're an embarrassment to me"; "you're a weakling"; "your behavior shames the family"; "I can't take you anywhere"; "I don't want to see your face"; or "You're going to turn out like your grandfather who was a real loser." Shaming words and phrases such as these are often used to provide the power needed to funnel children into accommodating to parental wishes and to gear themselves to pleasing the caretakers (more will be said about this topic later). How often children, when they make mistakes, are given labels such as "dumb," "sloppy," or "clumsy." If we know that the best defense against feeling shame is shaming another person – often through a "violent, fluorescent act," why do we continue to do this?

Helping children to maintain a strong sense of self and to feel successful is increasingly difficult, especially considering current trends in education. Years ago, it was commonplace for teachers to place children in reading, spelling, writing and math groups according to their ability. Group names such as "Peacocks," "Blue Jays," and "Buzzards", often were assigned to these groups of pupils. As you can imagine, or possibly remember yourself, the groups with the appealing names, such as the "Peacocks," were the higher-ability groups, while the "Buzzards," or groups with the less appealing names or connotations, were the lowest groups. Though this was mainly done for teacher convenience, to keep track of which students belonged within each group, the negative aspects of labeling students have been well documented. The labels seemed to become a long-lasting and self-fulfilling prophecy. A disproportionate number of students who were "Buzzards" in elementary school math continued to be lower than average throughout their academic careers and even into adulthood. Studies also showed similar results across all academic areas. (Example courtesy of Mr. Peter, an experienced high school teacher)

It is a fact that shaming very frequently takes the form of labeling, or name-calling. And it seems to be human nature that people often resort to calling others a name when the underlining problem is merely that *they don't understand* what the other person is feeling, and they *haven't taken the time to find out* who the other person is. We have seen this happen in medicine. Doctors called children "brats" until they discovered the diagnosis of attention deficit hyperactivity disorder. They called children "retarded" until it was discovered that there were many forms of Dyslexia. They called women various nasty words (unmentionable here) until premenstrual dysphoric disorder was added to the Diagnostic and Statistical Manual of Mental Disorders. Psychologists labeled people with "borderline personality disorder" who had numerous reactions of anger, until they discovered that many of these patients weren't being treated with empathic responses by their therapists, and perhaps had good reason to be angry without the doctor having to invoke a medical model to explain the patient's anger. Sometimes when a person is not feeling well because they are feeling deeply misunderstood or some of their most basic emotional needs are not being met, we need simply to look at these needs without attributing all their symptoms to a medical model. Much more about this will be described in the chapters that follow. But the point to be made here is that many children whose emotional reactions are not fully understood by the people in their environment receive *labels* early in their lives. These labels are carried by the child into adulthood and cause feelings of shame that resurface throughout life, especially during moments of crisis – those moments that Dave and I define as "shouldn't have done that" moments.

An example is a very intelligent male patient of mine in his mid-50s who is still tormented by the word "lazy." He is a kind and thoughtful person who grew up in a family that feared for financial security. They projected a lot of their own anxiety onto him and planted the word "lazy" in his head. This word still haunts him every time he feels he might be faltering in meeting a professional expectation. I must mention that, to the outside observer, he is a very busy and high-functioning lawyer who keeps long hours, is extraordinarily capable, well- educated, and professionally competent, but he still fights to keep the label "lazy" out of his mind during crises of stress or exhaustion. A label given to a child can be like a mark branded onto the hide of a cow – the mark becomes a part of one's skin, so to speak, and one takes for granted that it is a part of the self, often until the skin is examined closely with a caring therapist or even a loving mate or friend. The hopeful news is that even tattoos can be removed! And, the refreshing aspect of the Dave movies is that, despite all sorts of "flub-ups," no one ever gets branded with a name or label.

Shame spreads like an infection, infiltrating the pores of the child's self (the petals of his flower, to extend our metaphor) as his personality strives to emerge. Shame "gums up" and clouds over creativity like pus forms over a wound. And left unchecked, shame can spread to infect other potential buds of the self.

Since shame feelings are so painful, we may not be able to spot them right away. The infection can spread insidiously within a person before another person discovers it, eclipsing other positive feelings and strengths the self could be developing. The simple truth is that, as with a plant fungus, if shame feelings cannot be revealed, they cannot be exterminated. If left to perpetuate, shame feelings dwarf growth.

To extend our metaphor, to fight back we must pull out all the fungicides and insecticides we have in our armamentarium. We must seek to rid our precious plants and budding tendrils from the destruction of shame and guilt which act like burrowing worms, suffocating fungi and insidious tiny insects – all with the potential to break down the micofibers of a growing self. We have the tools. We have the chemistry. We have the will.

No plant can grow strong and tall with its structure weakened by holes created by shame. How different the lives of so many individuals could be if the forgiving mantra "Oops! *You* shouldn't have done that!" or the self-forgiving mantra "Oops! *I* shouldn't have done that!" could fortify and fertilize the soil in which we all grow. If this mantra permeated our atmosphere, wouldn't our society's propensity for ill will and contempt be lessened? And, as a natural corollary, isn't it fascinating to speculate how different our world might be if this enabled more individuals to let go of shame or resentment, move on with their dreams and live up to their own God-given potential?

*No labels* are given in the Dave movies. To ensure long-lasting success and a feeling of comfort and self-worth, why do we need to label at all?  Why pay attention to others' labels of our children, or ourselves, when we can build our own inner sense of worth.  The character Dave teaches children that it's OK to make errors.  Dave also shows us that different people have different abilities, and that not being *great* at everything is normal and healthy.  Through his movies, we see that even though Dave wants to be good at a variety of skills, more often than not, some mishap befalls him.  After all, we can't all be professional monster truck drivers, construction workers and demolition experts.  The fact that Dave tries these new experiences, has fun, can absorb a crisis and move on is an important message for us all.

To condense the BIG message of Our Little Text, Dave and I feel that the way to success is to confront shame with **P.R.I.D.E.:** **P**ositivity, **R**esilience, **I**ntegrity, **D**iscipline and **E**nthusiasm.  The mantra "I shouldn't have done that" integrates all five aspects of the **P.R.I.D.E. Factor**™.  First, it acknowledges that something "shouldn't have happened"; it does not deny, condone, or minimize that painful event.  It does *not* convey the attitude that "anything that happens is OK."  Dave, in all his "I shouldn't have done that," takes responsibility and accountability for his own action or problem.

The bedrock of healing is being able to acknowledge the pain and damage done from any injury.  Dave first admits the unfortunate occurrence, shares his pain out loud (often with at least one trusted friend such as Becky), and puts the feeling into words:  "I shouldn't have done that."  His doing this helps his audience connect with how universal the feelings of hurt are.

No matter what happens to him, Dave exhibits the attitude that one can be responsible for facing an injury and going on with the course of life. He can then disengage from the injurious event and ultimately take responsibility for making new forward-looking choices and for starting to make things better and more successful. He agrees with Alan Patton that "...any tragedy is not that things are broken. The tragedy is that they are not mended again."

Even when a really BIG mistake is made (as when Dave destroys a building by hitting the wrong lever while operating a large demolition machine), Dave isn't devastated or incapacitated by shame. He can see the event as something he *did* – that he should not have done – not something about *himself* that was flawed.

In *There Goes a Garbage Truck*, Becky pushes the wrong lever, all the garbage dumps out, and she and Dave have to start their collection route all over again. Dave says, "You shouldn't have done that," and they immediately get back to business and *re*collect all the garbage again! Whether it is public humiliation (such as being pushed over by a fire hose in front of the whole fire company, or being accidentally pulled up in the air by a crane hook on a construction site) or more private frustrations (such as running out of gas on his motorcycle trip, or getting lost on a freeway because the map had been read upside down), no one gets stuck in blame – neither self-blame, nor blame toward the other. They may vent and let off steam, but *no one gets stuck in self-degradation, self-condemnation, vengeance or victimhood.*

These video examples provide excellent models for both children and adults, illustrating the regulation of shame and guilt feelings and the process of self-forgiveness and forgiveness of others. Even when Dave runs over his father's car in *There Goes a Monster Truck*, he can continue to go on with life's adventures. When I showed this video to a group of priests whom I treat, one priest pointed out that this is the attitude with which Jesus lived his own life. He refused to get all tangled up with grievances and vengeance when he encountered sinners. Instead, he instructed them about how to live a better life, how to correct mistakes, and encouraged them then to move on with life. How different a model this is than our world seems to follow now, with so much preoccupation with revenge, victimhood and retaliation.

In our culture today, it seems that people would almost rather die than admit they've made a mistake. How different Richard Nixon's presidential legacy might have been if he had just been able to admit he made a mistake. He would have enjoyed much more compassion from the public, because we all make mistakes. It is a part of our shared humanity. But instead of admitting our mistakes, we seem stuck on shaming ourselves, and shaming other people. For shaming is a way of assigning superiority and inferiority, and somehow, that seems to be more comfortable for people than asserting our common humanity. Over 30 years later, many people still have not forgiven President Nixon.

We can all think of international stories of persistent "non-forgiveness" and probably interpersonal stories of non-forgiveness. Yet, Christopher Peterson, a psychologist at the University of Michigan, says, "Forgiveness is the trait which is the most strongly linked to happiness." He adds, "It's the queen of all virtues and probably the hardest to come by." Researcher Fred Luskin says that when we hold onto what he calls a "grievance story of injury," it can influence the rest of one's life including longevity and health. According to Luskin, "the key to forgiveness is trying to not take 'too personally' the injury." And this is the beauty of the Dave movies. Despite the defeats, irritabilities, setbacks, everyone resumes "full sail" without being cast back on poor self-esteem or shame at the moment of crisis.

All too often, in my practice I see people who can't release grudges and move forward. They take hurts very personally and feel that whatever event happened devalues their worth as an individual. The inspirational key to the Dave stories is that no one is personally devastated either by his own mistake or by the interpersonal conflict suffered. Even when Dave and Becky are crabby, or bicker, neither's spirit is crushed; they continue to enjoy each other's company and trusted friendship. Forgiveness and healing replace any feeling of catastrophe or personal judgment. In fact, after each "shouldn't have done that" incident, something new is learned that enables them to progress. One learns how to read a map, how to listen to the instructor, how to ask directions or how to start out by driving smaller trucks first. Something constructive is gleaned so the negative event is less likely to recur and there is progress beyond the hurt or disappointment.

And it was the relief of the emotionally charged situation dissipating that drew Grant and me to the Dave movies over and over again – how often "real life" glitches don't work out so smoothly. Feelings get hurt; people get disappointed; we do something we're mortified about; our feeling of stress is high, and a frequent response to a feeling of crisis or stress is the "fight or flight" response. This "fight or flight" response is a primordial response that goes back to the animal kingdom. A stressful, negative event occurs, and the body reacts by releasing stress chemicals to the perceived dangers. These chemicals cause discomfort in both the mind and body that are actually the same feelings, as one would have if a tiger were attacking. Blood vessels constrict; blood pressure rises; the heart beats faster; the liver dumps cholesterol into the bloodstream; digestion is altered; muscles tighten; breathing becomes shallow; and blood flow is diverted to the center of the body. Subjectively, we feel miserably stressed and uncomfortable. But this is a normal reaction to a perceived danger. Our body's sympathetic nervous system is revving up to protect us, and this affects all of our internal organs. It should be no surprise that there is much research to demonstrate that when this happens often it can lead to a higher incidence of illness such as cardiovascular disease and cancer, as well as the compromise of our immune response (Luskin, p. XV).

So, what was relieving (both physically and psychologically) about watching the Dave movies is that there was always an absence of the "fight or flight" response, which researchers have found can continue negative physiological changes related to physical illness and anger due to shame reactions. Simply put, all characters bounce back, the show goes on, and everyone's physiological regulation returns to normalcy.

So not only is it good for your emotions to "let go" after a negative event, it may actually *save your life* to internalize Dave's mantra "shouldn't have done that" – and learn to move beyond.

Protecting one's body from the destructive physiological changes of the fight or flight response requires releasing shame and forgiving the self, others, and often life.

In my work as a psychoanalyst for over 30 years, I have worked intensively with very good people who have been unable to release themselves from extraordinarily painful, even gnawing feelings of shame that have sometimes incapacitated them, making them feel like hiding from others, or at least inhibited them from a life of full spontaneity and self-expression. I have seen a huge amount of wasted time when people get stuck in blaming themselves or others for a mistake they made or an injury made to them. In addition, we are witnessing the phenomenon now in our culture whereby individuals who have experienced themselves as victims often become victimizers. People who cannot give up feelings of shame try to cope with their own shame by shaming others. A new term, "victo-terrorists," describes people who, feeling that they have been victimized, feel justified in becoming terrorists towards others. These people never move on with their lives, but rather, enshrine their victimhood by aggressing against other people.

As I mentioned before, people feel pressure to talk about feelings of guilt, because they expect to be able to confess and receive atonement. But to even mention a perceived defect or inadequacy in the self is excruciatingly painful. One priest in my practice whom I will call "Father B" had committed a mild sexual indiscretion (not involving a minor); he had had 10 years of treatment and no recurrence of the behavior. The time came to celebrate the 50th anniversary of his ordination, but he was too ashamed of what he had done 10 years ago to be able to celebrate this event.

Despite individual work with me and work in my group of priests, he could not get over the hump of the shame of his past indiscretion and proceed to enjoy this occasion. His one period of misconduct had dwarfed any other pride that he had in his 50 years of ministry. I was at a loss for how to help him, until I decided to bring in Dave's video *There Goes a Monster Truck* for my whole priest group to view. By the end of the video, all were chanting, "shouldn't have done that!" and giggling at the mantra. Father B. had his mind turned around. "Yeah," he said to the group shyly, "I guess I really shouldn't have done that, but I've learned a lot. I've come a long way. I'm restored now, and I'm ready now to have my celebration!"

This case is a perfect example of the magnificent healing power of Dave's mantra. The mantra is brilliant in that it separates the person from the behavior. What an important lesson for parents to know in raising children – how crucial it is to always separate what the child *did* from some defect in his or her character. I heard an example just the other day from an esteemed elder in my own family. This is a gentleman whom everyone always admired for his discipline, keen intelligence, dependability, perseverance, generosity and strength. In fact, he began university education at the age of 16 and went on, quite young, to run a major manufacturing company that employed 800 people. He was always very hardworking, studious, and responsible. In grammar school, he was the apple of the eye of particular teachers because of his good nature, kind personality, and dedication to his studies.

At the time that he entered high school, at age 12, his father insisted that he attend a large public school so that he could learn to interact with a broad range of people in preparation for taking on management responsibilities at the family company. As they drove up to the front door, the school looked enormous, imposing and frightening to this serious-minded and conscientious 12-year-old boy. He wanted so badly to do well and to please his father. They arrived at the school that morning in a brand-new car, fresh from the dealership. When the boy opened the door to venture out into this new experience, a flush came over his face and he threw up all over the leather interior and carpeting. His father gave him a hug, and the young man stiffened his lip, pulled himself together, and went on to face this new and intimidating challenge.

His father immediately took the car back to the dealership, where he was asked, "What happened! Who threw up?" The father, being a sensitive man, knew that the salesman would ridicule his boy if he told them of his son's school anxiety and what had really happened, and so he responded, "Well, you know those young kids. They try to act so grown up and so strong – all the kids were at our house last night, and they had a few too many 'Moron Sodas' – you know, those ice cream sodas with six scoops of ice cream in each – they were bragging about how big they were now and how much they could eat now that they were big high schoolers, and I guess he just ate more than his belly could hold."

What a wonderful, intuitive way of protecting his son from any labels about insecurity, weakness or shame, even when not in his presence! The implicit message was it's not that he should be called a fraidy cat, it's just that he "shouldn't have done that." (P.S. This was my own father and my grandfather!)

I've noticed that Dave's mantra "I shouldn't have done that" is also contagious. It is a phrase that has worked its way into my own family. My extremely active, exploratory, now 4-year-old little boy loves to jump on the bed late at night, showing off his (quite impressive) gymnastic talents, while my husband and I are on the brink of exhaustion. Usually, I, a child of the `60s, am a little more permissive than my husband, who is a more conservative, structure-oriented person.

But one night, even I had about had it (remember the chronic sleep deprivation?). This particular evening, Grant had jumped and jumped and jumped, doing somersault after somersault, proudly and enthusiastically exhibiting his seemingly inexhaustible prowess. Suddenly, to all of our surprise, he knocked over a huge glass of ice water, right onto the freshly pressed and recently changed bedsheets – managing to get the whole bed, pillow, mattress and two layers of blankets soaked through.

It was 11 o'clock at night. Mom, Dad and Grant all froze. A look of shock crossed all of our faces. It could have been one of those terrible scenes all families experience – the child cries; Dad scolds child for spilling water; Dad chastises Mom for not putting child to bed earlier; Mom snipes at Dad for scolding her; Mom, feeling guilty for not having her child under better control, snaps at Dad for scolding child and for scolding Mom; child cries because Mom and Dad are bickering (mostly out of frustration and exhaustion); everyone goes to bed mad and sad.

But, BINGO! This was not the case for us! Instead, within two seconds of the incident, we all relaxed, looked at each other with silly smiles and gleams in our eyes, and spontaneously chimed in together, "Shouldn't `a done thaaaaat…" Great giggling and laughter ensued, and everyone banded together to change the linens and go to bed happy! All feelings of shame were averted. Everyone's sense of personal pride was protected and/or restored.

As you continue to read this book, you will glean concrete guidance about how to inoculate yourself against shame and how to avoid "shame wrecks," that is, those experiences where the fight or flight response takes over, foreclosing all other choices and opportunities for future adventures. Instead, you will learn to protect yourself and your children against the chances of having these shame wrecks so that you can more easily go on with your life, after "I shouldn't have done that."

With our guidance, you will have internalized Dave's mantra "I shouldn't have done that"; "you shouldn't have done that"; or even "life shouldn't have done that." Then, having moved beyond the fight or flight response, and with your mind and body having a chance to be more relaxed and at ease, we will set forth the steps to help you to begin to reassemble your success attitude.

You will learn to activate the **P.R.I.D.E. Factor**™. After insults, failures, setbacks, or any "shouldn't have done that" you can come to feel positive, resilient and enthusiastic again. No matter what comes along, true success is in the bounce back.

# CHAPTER 4

## Vitality: Work at What You Love

The philosophy that has guided Dave's own personal life, and that has inspired his work and career, is the idea that the true goal of life is to achieve a meaningful, happy, and vital sense of self.

Vitality is the power to live and develop your unique physical, spiritual and mental energy – your personal sense of strength and style of being alive. No other person can set, or impose, an external program or template onto your life. Instead, you must dedicate yourself towards finding whatever direction, goals, or attachments will give you a sense of vitality and aliveness. If your life is constructed to meet primarily external goals, especially those assigned to you by someone else, you will very likely be left feeling unhappy, deadened, depleted, bored, and in a state of *ennui*. Then you are not, by definition, living a successful life.

Personally, I love what I heard Dave express: "The most enjoyable times in life are when you create fantasies and are disciplined enough to see them through to fruition." And this message is clearly conveyed over and over again in Dave's movies. The characters in the *Real Wheels* series make their dreams come true by learning to drive all sorts of huge, dauntingly complicated vehicles. As a psychoanalyst, I think the message of hope to make dreams come true is thrilling for both children and adults. It might very well be one of the reasons that watching the Dave movies holds such power over so many.

Contemporary psychoanalysts respect the fact that different activities will bring different people a sense of vitality. These activities can vary greatly from individual to individual. For this reason, individual differences must be respected and honored. For some, vitality comes from getting married, having a white picket fence around one's house, and raising a family; for others, it comes from being able to build a custom airplane and fly it. For some, it is mastering a musical instrument. For others, it is being able to live a solitary life in a cabin, writing a great novel. For still others it is solving mathematical problems. It is these idiosyncratic differences that bring so much diversity and interest into our world.

In fact, contemporary mental health professionals no longer measure health chiefly by external markers such as "the ability to hold down a job," or "the ability to keep a long-term, relationship," because we now recognize the importance of the condition of the individuals *internal* state as well. For example, I see many patients who have worked with determination, but cheerlessly, for goals that are not their own, and come to me, depressed, with the question: "Is that all there is?" One very attractive, well-off woman with a husband who adored her, came to me and said, "I have everything in my life, but I feel like the 'champagne has gone flat', there are just no more bubbles inside. Please help me find out what's missing."

When I interviewed Dave's sister, Pat Hood, she told me that she and Dave were influenced by their parents and grandparents to take the lead in finding out where their *own unique* talents lay and to be all that they themselves could become. Dave's mother said, "We always let Dave make early decisions on the simplest things, letting him choose what he wanted to do, wear or buy." How fortunate a background, and how sad that more children do not have this explicit permission to look inside themselves for their own personal goals and direction.

To return to the example of my 93-year-old patient mentioned in the introduction of this book, one of the most likely reasons for the success of her children (and grandchildren) was that this woman had intuitively created an atmosphere in which there was a deep interest in, and value placed on, who each person *was* in the family. In terms of the flower metaphor, this family maintained a curiosity about the individuality of each child, allowing him to grow into his own form and shape, and providing nourishment toward that end. Because each child was very different (in personality and in his innate talents and abilities), much of the parental work involved "tilling the soil," and "clearing out the rubble" so that both parent and child could bear witness to whatever form would evolve.

Some scholars, working more directly in the field of spirituality, have likened Dave's philosophy about vitality to the injunction of the book title *Follow Your Bliss* (Hal Zina Bennett & Susan J. Sparrow, 1990). Entertainer Danny Kaye (1913-1987) put it more colorfully: "Life is a great big canvas; throw all the paint on it that you can." Psychoanalysts such as Winnicott and his followers refer to this concept as living according to the needs of one's "True Self" (in contrast to the "False Self"). He is talking basically about being comfortable in one's own skin.

The important point here is that many psychoanalysts today find their offices populated with patients who, to the outside observer, "have it all." These people (so-called "successful"), viewed externally, have attained high levels of financial, material, educational, or other achievements – yet they often remain in excruciatingly painful psychological distress. Their depression is not based on guilt, or anger turned inward, as is often the assumption. Rather, it is a depression based on feelings of internal emptiness, depletion, or alienation from themselves. It is a terribly daunting, almost haunting, feeling, and an ordinary outside observer may have difficulty empathizing with (considering the person's external assets and achievements). But, close analysis of these patients' lives inevitably reveals a life of successful accommodation to the goals and desires of some other person (most frequently a parent or caretaker) that has ignored the needs of their individual True Self.

The 3,000 miles between us has collapsed and I know Dave personally now. I have observed firsthand that he, himself, exudes a sense of vitality – the earmark of a healthy sense of self. His sister, in fact, told me that Dave has always had a natural gift of humor that he could rely on to get through adversities. And his mother told me, "He learned very fast to talk and to walk and I do not believe he has ever stopped expressing himself." So, I guess it should have been no surprise to me that working together on this book would become the vitalizing experience it has been for me.

In addition to his personal enthusiasm, it is Dave's conscious philosophy about vitality and revitalization that has facilitated his success. In his personal journals, Dave has put some of these philosophies into words. He has also studied the work of others who have lived lives filled with vitality, and he has made efforts to keep these people consciously in his mind as role models. Dave sums up, very simply, his own core essence when he says: "I am going to live until I die."

And, despite the ups and downs in his movie stories, and some in his own personal story, for Dave there is a bounce in every ounce. The energy in his handshake, the emphasis in his voice, the life in his smile and hugs, are outward invisible signs of his own personal philosophy about bouncing back and aliveness. In our long hours of talking he told me about the importance of discovering what provides authentic enthusiasm and putting himself into the things he, himself, genuinely enjoys and cares about. And he believes in thinking carefully about what these things are and in making careful choices about where to commit his resources – be they time, energy, money, love or creativity. Because he has given careful thought about what is important to him, we can see a visible purposeful, energetic vitality to what he does. The brightness and hopefulness which Dave transmits in his movies, and by which he purposely conducts his life, can be captured in the word *vitality*. Vitality is about having life – or re-finding it. It's about having bounce, or bouncing back. It's about having hope, or re-finding hope. We know vitality when we have it. We know it when we don't have it. We can squish it in ourselves. We can squish it in our children. We can release it in our children and we can release it in ourselves. Dave seems to have it coming out of his ears. He lives by the West Point Cadet Maxim: "Risk more than others think is safe. Care more than others think is wise. Dream more than others think is practical. Expect more than others think is possible."

When I first met Dave, I must confess, I was nervous. I felt that I had had a long-term, informal relationship with him since I had watched him in all sorts of situations, during all sorts of antics and predicaments, over several years. My son and I had been right there with him as he interacted with all sorts of characters, and many daunting vehicles, and as he had negotiated many personal and interpersonal challenges. And our own involvement had gone on for years! I had watched Dave, myself, for at least 300 hours while trying to soothe my son (and myself) to sleep. Yet, in truth, I had never actually met him in person. Despite my sense of intimacy, we were, in fact, strangers! I wondered… was the Dave whom Grant and I had bonded with merely a TV persona? How would I "live" when all of my reaction patterns had been developed *vis a vis* the "Dave" my son and I had come to know so well in our own home?

But as soon as Dave and I met, at 10:30 p.m. after Dave's long day of performing two live stage shows in Providence, R.I., I knew within seconds that this was the Dave I had come to know and love in my home. In real life, backstage so to speak, he had the same twinkle in his eye, the same spring in his step, the same warmth in his smile, and the same radiance of self-confidence, self-worth and vitality. He showed all the signs, and had all the symptoms, of a man living his own life and enjoying it to its fullest.

Upon our first meeting, when my husband, Paul, and I went out to dinner with Dave and his gorgeous wife, Rebecca, actually I felt so relaxed and familiar that I began teasing with Dave in the prototype of an older sister to a younger brother (quite out of character with my customary professional demeanor!) I acted as if

I *had* known him for three years. I teased him as if our ages were 11 and 9, in fact. Suddenly I became flooded with embarrassment and wondered, "What will Dave now think of 'Dr. Munschauer'?" I remembered with a start that the real Dave had known me for less than an hour! His reaction was that of the fun-loving character he plays in the *Dave movies*. He said, "Oh, you shouldn't have done that," and then he laughed and gave me a hug. This incident attests to how close the real Dave is to the exuberant and vital "Dave" of his movies! And the joy and relief I felt in real life was the same sort of joy and relief that people feel vicariously when they watch these movies.

To return to the topic of healthy vitality, contemporary psychoanalysts describe "normality" as the ability to feel joy, pride in one's self and a sense of inner vitality. So it follows naturally that "success" is about seeking an *internal* sense of self-esteem, rather than relying on measures from the *outside* world. A corollary of this principle is that when people are in pain, good therapists know that the goal is not to *cure* them, but to help them discover their *own* potential, to find their *own* direction, and to return to the pursuit of their True Self. When they find the flexibility to reach toward their *own* sunlight, a sense of aliveness inevitably returns.

The point to be learned is that it is our own responsibility to keep track of what people, places, things and activities generate feelings of aliveness for us. Dave and I like to call this taking our "Vitality Pulse," or, for short, our "VP." It is an interesting exercise to do this as you go through your day in different situations, with different people and different activities. The VP is the indicator of whether or not we are generally going in the right direction for ourselves. Positivity theorist and psychologist Martin Seligman notes that "The happiest people in the world pursue personal goals and intimacy and judge themselves by their own yardsticks."

I had a patient in her 20s who was struggling to find her True Self. She was acutely aware of her desire to please her parents, not just for the sake of making them happy, but also because it made her feel so wonderful to see them pleased. She had moved along quite far on a career path that she knew in her heart was not her own. About nine months before graduation she dropped out of the program. Both of her parents were tremendously disappointed and she came to me in a great deal of conflict. She was so close to getting her degree, yet so far from achieving her dream.

She entered another university and registered for a totally different curriculum, well aware of her vulnerability to being influenced in her career choice by any academic mentor who might come her way that she liked and wanted to please. With tears in her eyes she looked up at me and said, "How will I know that I'm not just doing it again? How will I know this time that I am not just pleasing an advisor I like the way I did my father and that my path is still not my own?"

I told her that she needed to take her pulse. She looked at me as if I had gone crazy on her. "Literally?" she said as, with an incredulous look on her face, she pressed her fingers to her wrist. "Take my pulse?" At that point I explained the VP to her and spontaneously drew a picture of a thermometer.

I told her that once a week, in every class, she needed to fill in her thermometer. I advised her to make 50 copies of the thermometer marked with a temperature gauge on it and tuck it into her class folder and carry a red marker with her. Then, at the end of the semester, her assignment was to add up the temperatures. Whichever class gained the highest readings were the classes that gave her the most vitality. Apologetically, I said to her, "I'm a doctor, I guess that's why I chose a thermometer. If you have a different idea about some gauge that suits your True Self better and that would indicate a quickening or excitement, by all means choose your *own!*"

A few days later the patient called me very excitedly and left a message on my answering machine. She said, "Dr. Carol, I am so excited! You know how I love playing the piano. I really did not like studying all this science and biology that my father wanted me to. I really *don't* want to be a doctor. I want to keep studying the piano and maybe also the violin. What about the *metronome*? I could use the markings on the metronome as the gauge of my Vitality Pulse. I'm so excited about this, I can't wait to see you next time and talk more about it!"

I had a patient once who was a mariner who measured his Vitality Pulse through an image he knew well: that of a bell book, one that is used to document propulsion of a ship's motor at sea. When he would take on a new project, he would keep track of his feelings... Did he feel full steam ahead? Half steam ahead? Slow ahead? Stop? Half-stern or full stern? When he knew he was full steam ahead, he knew he was really excited about something. When he knew he was full stern, he knew he was in reverse. Whether it is a Geiger counter, a tachometer, a speedometer or a thermometer the closer the symbol comes to a symbol of your *own*, the more effective it will be for indicating to you when *your* Vitality Pulse is going up.

Dave's movies for children are replete with examples of his value of putting time and energy into what raises his VP and generates personal joy. In *Real Adventures: That's How They Do It! Chocolate.* Dave, as Professor Hoody, goes through all sorts of machinations to get a huge candy bar. When he gets back to his island home, his friend, the monkey, works almost as hard to get his own treasured coconut. Dave likes chocolate; monkeys like coconuts; neither tries to impose his taste on the other.

This attitude of respect for individual differences is the main ingredient in the development of a child with a success attitude. Parents must refrain from the temptation to use their children to accommodate their own needs or to fulfill their own dreams. They must stay attuned to the individuality of their child and work to nourish and foster the development of the child's own particular nature. We are not trying to be judgmental about parents here. It is very difficult, especially when one is blessed with a child who has particular strengths and talents that the *parent* values and wants to develop, but that the child shows no interest in pursuing. It is in these cases that it is very difficult for parents to allow their child to follow their own heart and their own spirit. Clinical experience shows that children who are pushed into areas for which they might have ability, but which are not "of their heart," lead lives filled with feelings of emptiness and depression. Avoiding this outcome is all a matter of staying aware of the factors that promote vitality.

We all know stories of parents who often, unwittingly, squash the true selves of their children by their own need to live vicariously through the child's talents and gifts. The prototypical example is the child pushed into hobbies, activities and even lifelong careers by his parents. Often, parents use children to fulfill unrealized dreams of their own. Maybe it was a fantasy of being famous, rich, or athletic, that drives a parent to push children in a direction they may not otherwise choose. All of us have heard stories of overbearing "stage moms" and "Little League sports dads." These stories usually center on the parents' aggressive nature, but rarely do we hear how this affects the child.

Ideas also can be encouraged to sprout, or they can be squished. To paraphrase an old quotation: it is intriguing to think about how many great novels may have been squashed in French cafes. Creative ideas can be seen as flowers, which are either nurtured to develop or snuffed out from their beginning sprout. I find myself attracted to the logo of the video cartoon *Noggin* (BDC 2003) which sometimes shows actual *leaves* and *branches* coming out of the head. What a wonderful metaphor for the potential within ourselves and within our children – a potential which is all there just waiting for nourishment.

Some time ago, I treated a rather artistic young man who was the only boy in a family of six siblings. His father had been a sergeant in the Army, and had always regretted that he had not moved further up in the military ranks and had a military career. The family was a very close one with a lot of love and regard for each other, and this boy, in particular, as the only son, had always had an extremely close relationship with his father. Father and son came to me in great turmoil with what they described as their "first conflict." The son had decided that he wanted to leave the military and pursue an artistic career. He had already begun to gain recognition in New York City for his work and had received honors both academically and in the marketplace.

The father felt tremendous hurt and betrayal. All he ever wanted was for his son to become a Merchant Marine officer. With tears in his eyes, he looked at his son and me and said, "All I want to do is die knowing that you are wearing those ensign bars and then I would know that you will be secure; you'll be taken care of; your career will be secured." He continued, "If you just stay in for one more year, you can do it. Why are you stopping now? I can't understand it." The pain that was in the room as father and son worked this through was enormous. Luckily, there was a long history of love and respect between them, and father came to understand his son's need to live a vital life that expressed the needs of his own innate personality. The father even said, "I guess what would really be important to me on my *deathbed* is knowing that my son feels *alive*." But often the results are not so happy.

What is refreshing about the Dave character is that he explores many different hobbies and activities, demonstrating a wide range of exciting careers. He can make all of these look both valuable and achievable. And, at the end of each movie, someone who loves his career tells the kids that "You too can be a (whatever...), if you work hard and stay in school." Dave also tells kids where they can go to learn more about the vehicle that has just been featured in the movie. Dave actually got *me* interested in trucks! Since watching the movies, I have noticed, with interest, more vehicles, of all different shapes, sizes, and features than I have ever noticed before in my 55 years. And, I can talk about them! Furthermore, it is really fun to hear my lawyer-husband brag that his "non-outdoorsy," traditionally feminine wife took him to a truck show!

Sharing an open mind, valuing diversity of interests and, most of all, communicating alternatives to your child allows him to bloom and stretch his branches with flexibility. Watching your child explore various aspects of the world will not only help your child, you'll be surprised at how your relationship will bloom as well. A parent who imposes an overbearing agenda on a child is like a gardener who plants a flower that has the potential to "grow big" into a small, constricting pot. Eventually, the flower's roots have nowhere to go, the nutrients are used up, and in essence, the blooms of the flower will shrivel, fade, droop over, and eventually, die.

Living according to the directives of our True Self must be the focus of our adult lives as well. Christopher Morley says, "There is only one success – to be able to spend your life in your own way." With so many pushes and pulls and competing factors for our time and attention, staying centered on our *own* VP is the key. And after a crisis or setback our VP becomes our guiding light.

But this guiding light requires kindling from other people. In our time, the term "find yourself", has become a glib expression; it sounds like a solo mission on a desert island. The image eclipses all the needs a person has that must be provided from the environment in order to "find" or have a self. These critical environmental needs – or nutrients – will be explained further in Chapter 5. For now, it is enough to say that you can't find your True Self alone. It is a mission that we can accomplish only with the support and help of people who are, or whom we can rely on in memory that have been, important to us in the past. It can even be just one person. But what makes us human is that we are born in connection with other people, and we remain in connection with other people from birth until death. This is in fact our only innate drive, our only innate wired-in instinct.

A perfect example of this deep personal connection can be found in Dave's relationship with his beloved grandfather, Floyd, who lived to be 92. Dave bravely gave the eulogy at his funeral. Floyd worked in a sawmill in the Columbia River Gorge town of Stevenson in Washington State. He was given the opportunity to move up to management of the company. He preferred and very much loved to work with his hands in the workshop. He turned the promotion down, Dave spent many pleasurable hours working beside his grandfather, sharing their common interest in woodworking and treasuring the opportunity to work by his side. Dave's attachment to his grandfather was deep, and his grandfather taught Dave the strong belief and value: "Do what you *love*, and you will be successful."

This advice has guided Dave's career and captures his personal connection with his grandfather and his enthusiasm for his pursuits. Working at what he loved influenced Dave as a young teenager to have a job at a radio station and it's the same philosophy now that guides him in writing, producing, directing and acting in his movies for children. Now, Dave will begin a series on public television. It seems that every 10 years, Dave finds another area of WORK

+ LOVE = SUCCESS proving, and validating, over and over his grandfather's wisdom, coupled with his loving relationship with a father whom he described as accepting of his True Self and "laid-back" nature: Dave's flexibility and movement was blessed with parental sanction.

"Work at what you love", means enthusiastic discipline, or putting energy into those things that make you feel alive, or vital. Psychoanalysis calls what Dave's grandfather was modeling the True Self. The True Self has to do with the form the flower would take if allowed to develop naturally – if provided with adequate sunlight, soil, water and support from all sides by its environment. By contrast, the False Self is the term used when a self is forced to grow in a distorted way to accommodate to whatever nourishment its environment provides. For example, if a parent is inclined to nourish the talents the parent values and not the talents his developing child values, the self of the child will naturally grow towards that nourishment, forfeiting the growth of the branches in his own preferred direction due to lack of nutrients there. As one patient of mine said, "It feels so good to please my father. He's excited when I please him; I love the feeling when I please him. I know what I really want to do with my life, but it feels so good to please him that, at those moments, I forget it. It is only later on that I feel such sadness and despair that I'm not living my own life." She continued with tears running down her face, "I really don't want to be a physicist. I want to be a writer."

Intuitively aware of the True Self/False Self dilemma, but unaware of the technical terms, 10 years ago Dave said, "Very few people were given any applicable advice for getting started on the path to success, and very few young people are encouraged to go inside their *own* heads to find material with which to dream big." Maybe Secretary of Defense Donald H. Rumsfeld was thinking the same thing when he said in May 2003 at the commencement of the U.S. Naval Academy, "Don't be afraid to think for yourself, to take risks, and to try new things. Recognize that you may meet resistance along the way. Expect it. But don't be dissuaded. Progress in life generally comes from those who swim upstream."

As Dave actualized his dreams to become a performer, his confidence increased and any traces of shyness he had as a child (yes, even Dave was shy at times) evaporated. As his True Self came through, the admiration he received bolstered his self-confidence, and continued to vitalize him. And Dave had a real boost in self-confidence when he moved to Southern California in 1985 to co-host and produce the highly rated television show *PM Magazine* in San Diego. He felt like a "rocket that had finally reached orbit" on his way to achieving his long-range goal of performing nationally. And, now unobstructed, the path of his True Self continues to follow its own trajectory. Dave's show *Real Wheels* now airs on more than 60 public television stations across the country and that number is expanding as he enters his second season.

Dave's career has flourished mainly because of his philosophy that people need to appreciate and develop their *individuality* at all stages of life. He believes so strongly in working at what you enjoy that he frequently says that he feels as if he is "playing" at his work. He can say that because his work was selected by his True Self. The emergence of Dave's career, and his joy in it, validates the words of Henry David Thoreau: "We are constantly invited to be who we are."

Dave's sister said, "Our parents encouraged both of us to be independent and they said we could do anything we set our minds to. Dave seemed to use humor naturally to cope with any adversity." And Dave's mother describes the early origins of the True Self that she saw in Dave: "His early entertainment started very early. He always booked a party on Halloween, usually a costume party; he loved to dress up in funny things and make people laugh. When he went to school in first grade, his first big part was dressing up as a ghost for the school Halloween party. He jumped up on the desk, and got really carried away with his part in his white sheet and stole the show. By Christmas, he was ready to play Santa Claus. I dressed him up, and off he went – thinking he would just entertain his class – but the principal saw him and had him go around to all the eight grades with his 'Ho, ho, ho, merry Christmas.' I believe that this was when the 'entertainment bug' bit. He loved the applause! In the fourth grade, a group of his friends and he went around to other schools and entertained, lip-syncing to Alvin and the Chipmunks and square dancing."

As we can see, Dave found out early what he liked to do best and has kept his goals planted deeply in his mind. He strives to foster this with his own children. He adds, "After parents do the job the best they can in the early years, its wonderful to sit back and watch their children perform in the profession they alone have chosen."

I once met a woman who had been distressed because her son

had a habit of disassembling every musical instrument that she was given. Because she was a musician by avocation, the house contained a saxophone, a custom guitar, an electronic keyboard and all sorts of other instruments. She would play them semi-professionally, and he was learning to play them. Her son was becoming a gifted musician, but he also had an intense interest in how things worked. Frequently she would come home from her job as a social worker and find the expensive instruments disassembled all over the floor. The last straw came when she arrived home one day and the brand-new upright piano was in pieces on the floor!

Because she was an enlightened woman, and thanks to her background in social work, she didn't go into a meltdown, but she consulted a psychologist friend frantically asking, "What should I do?" The psychologist wisely asked her, "Would you consider your son creative?" She said, "Yes, actually he's very creative." So the psychologist advised her to "leave him alone." Although she was a tidy person by nature, she sucked in her breath and vowed to learn to tolerate the disarray so that her son could work out the part of himself that he was expressing. Now he has a contract to write music for Disney.

This illustration is an example of a parent with an unusual capacity to both tolerate and promote the evolution of the child's True Self, perhaps, we might hypothesize, because of the similarity of her son's True Self to that of her own. Most children, no matter how creative, do not necessitate their parents' being quite so flexible. But the example shows the payoff for both parent and child when the trajectory of the True Self can be permitted.

In contrast, with the False Self, psychoanalysts often deal with people who are living in depression because they have over-accommodated to the goals and desires of another person – most commonly parent figures. These patients can be identified by their lack of self-confidence. They lack a certain "*joi de vivre*." A very famous psychoanalyst Heinz Kohut, founded the field of self psychology in part because he wondered what happened to the spontaneous enthusiasm that children exhibit in the early stages of life. More recently, psychoanalyst Carol Gilligan in *The Birth of Pleasure: A New Map of Love* (2003) studied the diminishment of emotional accessibility in boys at about age 6 as they become acculturated in school and have to accommodate to stereotypical role models in our culture that demand that boys suppress their emotion.

Psychoanalyst Bernard Brandschaft has written a great deal about the False Self which he believes can be identified by symptoms of depression and depletion. For Dr. Brandschaft, these symptoms stem from what he terms "pathological accommodation," or that is, living one's life in compliance with the needs of other people. Examining the childhood of these people reveals that there has been little flexibility offered or interest in the emergence of their True Self and that, in order to survive and find nourishment, their flower had twisted and contorted by accommodation to get supplies. No wonder it is in distress.

Another example of this pathological accommodation is a young doctor ("Dr. G") whom I treat and who is a gifted and talented man in many areas. He is also a handsome, articulate and kind person.

Dr. G's parents were immigrants and feared that he would never be able to earn enough money to become financially secure. Because of their *own* financial anxieties and their *own* fears for his financial future, they actively discouraged any childhood interest their son had in fish and marine biology (since, from their perspective, scientists didn't earn much money). Instead, beginning at a very young age, they subtly, and then not so subtly, pushed him into the field of medicine. They urged him to volunteer in hospitals throughout grammar school and high school, and discouraged his interest in any experiences that would have fed his curiosity about fish breeding patterns. Because of his keen intellect, Dr. G excelled academically and graduated with a medical degree at an early age.

Dr. G was brought to my attention during an acute emotional breakdown, which he had the weekend he "succeeded" in receiving his medical degree. From the start of his treatment, his conflict was clear. On the heels of graduation, feelings of deflation, depletion, and loss of vitality overtook him like the undertow of a tidal wave. Dr. G's True Self had been suffocated during years of study, as he devoted his life to providing his parents with the security about his future that *they* needed and that they impressed so heavily upon him.

Our therapy began, quite understandably, with Dr. G's fear that I, too, would be using him for my own needs. He expressed discomfort that my fee was designed to exploit so that I could enlarge my house and that the frequency of our sessions had more to do with my own need for money than with any diagnosis or therapy. Because of his intelligence and insight, Dr. G was able to address these issues with me directly and our work together deepened rapidly.

He said, "I am caught between Scylla and Charybdis. Scylla was to accommodate, and then resent it because I collapse my True Self, and Charybdis is that I honor the interests of my True Self and get hurt and feel ashamed. Every time I feel I'm doing something *I want* to do I have an internal feeling that it's not sanctioned, and every time I feel like I'm doing something *I should* do I get depressed." I have never heard the True Self/False Self dilemma explained so well:

"Will I still have 'relationship privileges' if I don't synchronize myself

with what someone I love wants?"

Our work slowly enabled him to grieve his lost opportunities as a child and young adult to "work at what he loved." He discovered ways of incorporating his lifelong interest in fish with his commitment to medicine by focusing part time on aspects of biological research, which can apply to both fields. As he was child-free, he was able also to take long sabbaticals doing oceanographic research.

Another patient of mine, "Ms. Bond," was not so lucky on the path to realizing her True Self. She had come from a family funeral business that spanned generations. This business had been the nucleus of the family's prestige, reputation and considerable prosperity. From an early age, Ms. Bond's skills had been incorporated into the business. She was a gracious and diplomatic individual by nature, and her interpersonal skills were an asset to her employment. For these attributes she was rewarded generously, both monetarily and in terms of increased goodwill for the business in the community. By the time Ms. Bond was 45, she was president and sole stockholder of the business, which had seven branches, all of impeccable reputation, across the county.

Ms. Bond came to me with problems of alcohol abuse, multiple psychosomatic complaints, and dependence on prescription pain medication. Because she enjoyed so many comforts in her life, it was painful for her to address the roots of the anguish she was facing. Eventually, with my support, she came to realize that, at base, the goal of community prestige and financial prosperity had not been *her* priority, but that of her ancestors, most of whom had now passed on. In order to perpetuate the "family name," she had, from an early age, centered her life on the business and sacrificed many opportunities for exploring other aspects of life including personal relationships. Most dramatically, she had missed the chance to have her own biological child.

Our work in therapy focused on deep and painful feelings of loss, shame, depression and anger. At times there were thoughts of suicide, because Ms. Bond felt that her life, as she phrased it, "had *already* been snuffed out." After much anguish, soul-searching, prayer (Ms. Bond was a deeply religious woman), and deliberation, she chose to sell the business to some cousins.

Now independently wealthy, she began devoting her days to a children's charity. Soon, her vitality (VP) increased, and her depression lifted. Her feelings of deadness or being "snuffed out" were now gone, and she no longer needed to achieve a sense of aliveness artificially through stimulants such as drugs and alcohol. But, this process has been a long and hard road. It has been very painful to journey with her as her analyst. Had Ms. Bond's parents known, or had Ms. Bond become aware at some point, that true "success" was not a goal, but was the pursuit of the internal feeling of vitality, aliveness, and meaningfulness, her path might have been quite different.

In my work I have found that people who have "gone to the edge" and almost lost their balance, stop caring so much about what people think or say about them and live more spontaneously. I have seen this in people who have come close to successfully committing suicide or who have survived cancer or a major heart attack. Being granted a second chance seems to free them to become more internally directed, and to feel justified in discovering and following their own compass – it should have been their natural birthright from the beginning. An example is a patient of mine who has been a nun for 25 years. She was raised in a family where her mother became very ill when she was young. For this reason, it was understood in the household that everyone must "be quiet." The clear messages were: "don't express any strong emotion"; "keep everything calm"; "don't get anyone, especially mother, upset"; "pipe down!" This attitude soaked into my patient's pores so much that when she felt her call to religious life, she was drawn into cloistered living. Though she did not actually join a cloistered order, she lived most of her life in a religious community in the style of "keeping a low profile," tuning into the needs of others, holding back on expressing her own feelings and emotions, and suppressing any of her own strong reactions in front of other people.

As I worked with Sister Lee in therapy, I could see that underneath her neutral presentation was a very spirited, colorful, energetic and creative person, deeply conflicted about expressing that part of herself. She had strong ideals about social justice and about how people should be treated within her community, but the internal prohibition against "making waves" or putting anyone "out-of-balance" kept her, for the most part, demure and suppressed. She could feel her "red flags go up" when an issue touched her emotionally, yet you could never see such a reaction in her presentation.

About three years into treatment, Sister Lee was diagnosed with metastatic cancer. She went through a year of intense treatment that included surgery, chemotherapy, and radiation, leaving her out of work, with a great deal of time to reflect on herself, and reprioritize. During this time, as the chemotherapy tapered off, and the color returned to her face, she began to express to me that she thought that her True Self was to be more empathic in her opinions on social justice and issues concerning how people treat each other.

She had concluded that it might not be so catastrophic to "rock the boat" for a good cause. She acknowledged the effect of the atmosphere of her childhood home and thought consciously about how *she* wanted to comport herself in present day. She told me that with the years that she had left, she wanted to "make a few things right." And, she was also able to do some testing out in her community where she was delighted to find out that sticking up for herself didn't kill anyone! It was as if she had heeded the words of Abraham Lincoln, "If you want to avoid all criticism, don't do anything, don't say anything, don't be anything."

Luckily, the happenstance of one's parent's influence, or life's events, does not necessarily determine one's future. Even if you have led a life of accommodation to someone else's script, you can make choices now that can release you and promote revitalization. Following your Vitality Pulse can become a learned skill. Even if you do not see an analyst, with the help of a close friend and a true desire for introspection, you can get in touch with your own core values and gear your decisions towards actualizing them. In this process, you can find and validate your own unique skills, interests and abilities. You can decide what makes you feel alive. Entertainer/comedian Bill Cosby has said, "I don't know the key to success, but the key to failure is trying to please everybody."

Dave likes to quote William Earnest Henley, "I am the master of my fate; I'm the captain of my soul." He believes in this so strongly that he takes time to access "messages" from his "True Self" – a vital True Self which is always growing and developing. He quotes poet Diane Ackerman, "I don't want to be a passenger in my own life." And to ensure that this does not happen he goes away alone on a regular basis to commune in solitude with his self. While sailing or swimming, Dave tills his emotional garden. He tries to cultivate ideas that have been taking root in the back of his brain. He tills the soil and pulls out the weeds so that the flowers can grow more freely! Dave calls these "listening sessions," but what he is really doing is watching and respecting what is growing in his own inner garden. The point is that the idea of the True Self is so precious to Dave that he makes time to pay attention to the sprouts that are developing and to remove anything that is blocking new growth.

And to make way for new growth, there must be a balance in life between involvement and solitude. For, sometimes it is in solitude, in the moments of our deepest sleep or most random fantasies that ideas are able to germinate and take root, even out of our awareness. Dave has confidence that a self, unencumbered by mundane distractions, can sprout goals, almost subconsciously. If the mind is allowed to meander flexibly through the gardens of our subconscious it might even run into a sunflower – or a Jack in the Beanstalk. Isn't this what big dreams are made of?

I agree wholeheartedly. One never knows what will pop up in the lush and fertile greenery of the subconscious. When I was working on my doctoral dissertation, I labored to understand the year's worth of data I had collected. Try as I might, hour after hour, at my desk with my cat peering over my shoulder at my notes, I could not resolve the meaning of the data. Then I went to sleep and had a dream about two dark lines, as in a graph. One was a clear V-shape, the other was sort of a half rectangle. The next morning, I sat at my desk again in despair. Would I ever be able to analyze the results of this entire year of research? Unable to find any other way to think about my problem, I remembered my dream, and decided, on a lark, to see if my groups of subjects fit into either one of the graphic patterns that I had dreamed.

Suddenly, I was overwhelmed – the "V" design clearly illustrated one group, and the half rectangle differentiated the other group. Through statistical analysis, my results were at the .001 level of significance (which was highly significant), and I had my first publication!

Though I had been skeptical of people's claims that they could solve problems during sleep, this personal experience convinced me, beyond doubt that our minds are fertile places where miracles grow! Since then, I have not been surprised when I have had patients who have come to conclusions about issues in their life during their sleep. Now, as I continue to write, I count on this phenomenon by beginning my thoughts about a subject well in advance, and letting my mind work on its own, often while I am cleaning up my desk, vacuuming the rug, or preparing in other ways to "consciously think about" the project at hand. Likewise, the well-known English professor and writer Irving Massey is said to hear so much original music in his dreams that he has had to learn how to transcribe music in order to write down these unconscious musical creations.

In contrast, the False Self is not so creative and free. It is a desperate flower, leaning, for survival, towards whatever light source may be available. It does not have the luxury of focusing on self-actualization (Maslow), or inspiration, or thriving, or aliveness, or vitality. It is just trying to get whatever supplies are around in order to survive. To the outside observer, the flower is alive, but the form of the flower is not what it would naturally become if the light, and water, and fertilizer and other nutrients were plentiful and evenly distributed. And, if you ask the flower how it felt from the inside, it would say, "weak and hungry."

In closing this chapter, I want to reiterate that my years of clinical experience have taught me that no one's fate is cast in stone by one's past, one's parents, or even by the events in one's own life, no matter how defeating, discouraging, humiliating or traumatic they might seem. And the reason for this is that vitality is a renewable commodity that can be recharged, restored, renovated, or resurrected. Vitality is generated from the *inside*. It is like a pilot light that might go out in a storm, but can be re-lit or reactivated.

A friend of mine and contemplative Jesuit priest wrote the following poem which captures the renewable aliveness of the True Self. It generates vitality in me and I would like to share it here:

### THE BLOOD FLOWING THROUGH MY VEINS IS NOT A SHOULD

A new type, the doctor said, I can't find
any traces of guilt or supposed-to.
Let me look closer, magnify… Why, this is splendid,
well-rounded cells, flowing smoothly, indeed radiant.
You must feel, even see, differently.

Yes, I nodded, the body so light
and easy to move,
the sludge of ancient burdens,
like so much baggage,
dropped on the wayside.

As I look ahead, everything seems to glisten;
I follow an ease.

Ah! What's *that* like? He asked.

It's like the body and the earth suffused with vitality,

the arteries of life open and wide,

giving me fluency, the power to flourish.

I hear the voice of my own spirit and its resonances

in the world, my body echoing,

the blood rebuilding itself in resilience and beauty.

The doctor laughed. I could use a transfusion, he said.

Father Daniel Lusch, 2004

As you continue to read this book you will see numerous examples of people whose pilot light went out, so to speak, but for whom the light shone through again. These people, as Barry Manilow sang, "made it through the rain," and recouped their lives by acting according to their own heart's desire. Their flowers found an abundance of nutrients, where once all had seemed barren.

You will learn more about exactly how to renew your vitality and "bounce back" in the chapters that follow.

# **CHAPTER 5**

## NOURISHING VITALITY: THE FIVE PSYCHOLOGICAL FOOD GROUPS

The theme we have been establishing is that vitality (one's VP) indicates a healthy sense of self that can be built, and lost and regained again, despite the inevitable hardships, misfortunes, reverses, and adversities of one's life. In the last chapters we have focused on the meaningfulness of Dave's mantra "shouldn't have done that" and the importance that this mantra has for acknowledging the distress of loss, disappointment, life blows, misdeeds, imperfections, various plights and actual cataclysms. In human life, these events can range from fairly trivial things (such as stepping on the fork end of a rake and getting thumped on the head by the handle, as happened in *There Goes a Bulldozer*, to being paralyzed in a car accident or punished by the law for an act of financial wrongdoing).

Many people's lives remain stuck in a "shame wreck" because they can't progress beyond the "I shouldn't have done that," "you shouldn't have done that," or "life shouldn't have done that" stage. This was almost the case with the priest who was on the verge of ignoring the magnificent celebration of his 50 years of service as a priest because of a relatively small incident of misconduct 10 years before for which he could not forgive himself.

This chapter will focus on specific techniques for how to bounce back when an "I shouldn't have done that," or a "you shouldn't have done that," or a "life shouldn't have done that" event happens.

In five subsections, we will provide direction about how to raise children. But we will also define steps that adults can use when they need to bounce back from the inevitable ill fortunes, calamities, and even potential catastrophes that seem to be part of our shared human condition. This chapter will introduce you to the Psychological Nutrition Pyramid, which parallels the traditional Nutritional Food Guide Pyramid. We know that our physical diet should comprise portions of carbohydrates, lots of servings of vegetables and fruits, and some proteins, such as beans, meat and cheeses. The fats, oils and sweets should be eaten sparingly. In the Psychological Nutrition Pyramid, there are similar needed nutritional balances. In both pyramids, each individual "food group" provides some but not all of the nutrients you need daily. Health involves centering your diet on foods in the lower portions of the pyramid, and enjoying foods at the top of the pyramid more sparingly.

Just as a vital body thrives with nourishment from all five Food Groups, a vital psyche needs nourishment from all the Psychological Food Groups. It is worth emphasizing again that we need the same balance of food groups no matter what age we are, and that we never outgrow *any* of the needs we have.

In the first part of this chapter I will describe, with case illustrations, the characteristics of the nutritional food groups. The model should become easy to understand, interesting and appetizing to all readers. Dave and I have also included a blank Food Group Pyramid for you to begin to fill in as you read this chapter, because you and only you can determine what people, activities, ideas, places and interests energize your True Self. In the next chapter we will

# The Traditional Food Guide Pyramid

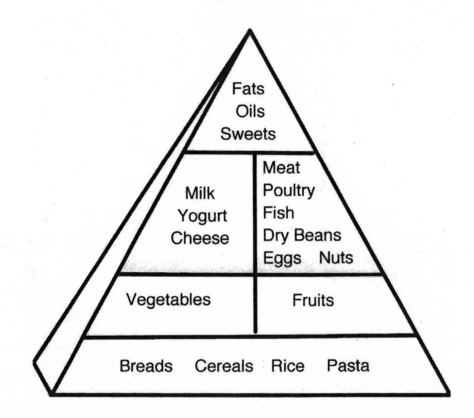

# The
# Psychological Nutrition
# Pyramid ™

Sparring

Twin-ship

Idealization & Heroes

Mirroring & Affirmation

Connectedness & Belonging

help you develop and fill in your own personal pyramid.

In the second part of the chapter, we will begin to help you learn to think about applying the Psychological Nutrition Pyramid to build up your own strength when life has delivered you a blow. These might be times when you have been "shame wrecked" or when you have suffered a loss, a reversal, a disappointment, or failure. It may be when you have had a reversal in your health, your employment, a personal relationship, or any other sort of disappointment or rejection. The purpose of this chapter is to let you know that you have hope. It is to expand your knowledge and begin to give you a sense of power, choice, and flexibility. You can restore your *self* if you are aware of the Psychological Food Groups. If you search your environment (or create your own environment) you will be able to revitalize and resuscitate yourself after disillusionments, mortifications, frustrations, letdowns, or even disasters. Perhaps some of them are even germinating right now.

Picture, for a moment, a flower that has wilted and is hanging down over its ornate pot, searching for a warming ray of sunlight peeking through a curtain. If only it could find the light, its fertilizer, the water. If only it could find it unencumbered, and unblocked, how would that flower begin to stretch and develop? With light and nutrients taken for granted, we could only imagine how its branches might take form. Dave and I want to remind you of something that you most likely have forgotten if you are stuck in an injury or shame wreck – you have more power than a potted plant! You can *move* yourself towards the very light and specific nutrients that you need to develop your own potential. It is never too late to twist around, grow in a different direction, to thrive and bear fruit again.

Successful and vital people learn to regain their initiative and strengthen themselves – even if their bloom has faded or waned, shriveled and withered, or even been traumatically stomped on. It is never too late, and one can make up for lost time. My dear friend Grace once said to me at a time when I had lost this perspective and was in a deep state of mourning from which I thought I would never recover, "Carol, there is a light at the end of the tunnel; you just can't see it from where you're standing." Although Grace passed prematurely from this life, she is a person who will always be part of my internal support system. Every time I feel discouraged, I remember these words and hear her suggestion in my heart now. When I can see no light, I try to get up, stand somewhere else, and take a different look.

Unlike a flower, which is dependent on the happenstance of a passerby recognizing that it is wilting, you can *seek out* Psychological Food Groups. If the garden in which you are planted is not enriched, you can hire a new gardener, or even move to another garden. The Dave movies illustrate that Dave is in control. When he gets "wrecked," he acknowledges that the injury has occurred, changes his course of action, and continues on in a *new* direction to thrive. Not only has this been the theme of his movies, but it's also the theme of his personal life.

This chapter will describe the basic psychological nutrients needed to build strong children who will be resilient to shame. It will also help enable anyone to empower him or herself to bounce back after feelings of defeat. You will learn how to *use* the Psychological

Food Groups in your own life, even if it means making changes or readjustments to get the nutrition that *you* need to move forward and be successful as your True Self. There are always choices ahead; there are always new paths. There are always new gardens. You do not have to be stuck in a malnourished state with your only options being fight, flight, toxic stress hormones or other blights or infestations on your flower.

Let's begin with our pyramid. I suggest that you tear out the blank one provided towards the end of the book and begin to work along with this discussion. Dave and I will help you even more with this in the next chapter.

To introduce the Psychological Nutrition Pyramid, it can be said that it is obvious that anyone who is well fed with the right nutrition will enjoy a sense of well-being and health. Deprivation of nutrition, either physical or psychological, never makes people strong, and never inspires or motivates people. Whether we are 5 months, 15, 50, or 85 years old, we all have the same pyramid of psychological needs. They just differ in amounts, or rather, they differ as to which ones are in the foreground at a particular moment.

Psychologists influenced by Sigmund Freud, the founder of psychoanalysis, used to think that people were motivated by the "pleasure principle" and that their whole lives were spent trying to manage their sexual and aggressive drives. Contemporary psychoanalysts believe that the main thing people are searching for is not a discharge of sexual or aggressive impulses, but rather a feeling of belonging and connectedness to other people. This longing to be in relation continues throughout the life span, through all the stages of adulthood from infancy to senescence. It is the ingredient that ultimately defines us as human. Even if we are living alone on a desert island or in a remote cabin in the woods, we are still psychologically in relation to people whom we have internalized in our minds and hearts – those who have influenced, guided us, or helped us to become who we are – like, for me, my dear friend Grace.

The nourishment that a person can get from the environment is a crucial determinant of the core feeling of well-being and self worth. From childhood through adulthood the responsiveness, or non-responsiveness, of the environment, deeply affects our day-to-day feelings and state-of-mind.

For children to grow up having good self-esteem and a happy sense of themselves, it is essential that they receive certain kinds of responses (nourishments) from their environment – a certain atmosphere to grow up in that enables them to feel connected with, and responded to, in ways that become as basic to their psychological health as the Five Food Groups are to their physical health. Children need support for "the development of a positive self-image and an internal sense of control." (Herrenkohl, Herrenkohl & Egolf, 1994) Simply put, they need food for the development of the True Self.

The same holds true for adults. Human needs are basically the same across all ages. Though they differ in degree, they do not differ in kind. In order for adults to have, maintain, or re-establish, a sense of wholeness, peace, stability, and happiness, grown-ups also need support for the needs of their True Self and the psychological nutrition to maintain a positive self-image.

This chapter will focus on the kind of nourishment adults can provide for children and also for themselves to promote or restore psychological health. It is as simple as that. Because it's usually the responsiveness (or non-responsiveness) of people in one's life that maintains this sense of peace and vitality, or disrupts it, we can learn to watch ourselves carefully and to trace the ups and downs in our daily sense of self-esteem or well-being. By paying attention to our inner states, we can come to understand what nutrients we, ourselves, need and we can learn to become conscious of what nutrients those around us need.

It is this understanding that enables us to promote stability and well-being for ourselves and for those important to us. You will understand more about psychological nutrition (and deprivation) as you read and learn more about the five basic Psychological Food Groups. And we have the founder of contemporary self psychology, Heinz Kohut, M.D. and his followers to thank for the basic principles behind the Psychological Nutrition Pyramid.

We all know that sometimes we feel energized, expansive, and emotionally confident that "the world is our oyster." We want to be extroverted, to reach out and to connect with people; our "wheels are running smoothly." We want to express ourselves, or take a creative risk. We want to be expansive, to "strike out and make our mark." It is at these times that we can characterize ourselves as being strong or "psychologically well fed."

At other times, we feel weak, lethargic, withdrawn, and contracted. We may feel like hiding or shrinking into the woodwork – being a wallflower. We may feel nervous and insecure about our looks, our ideas or opinions. We may feel like staying close to home – not even calling our close friends. We may feel achy. We have a "bad hair day." As the old song by Lorentz, Hart and Richard Rodgers goes, we feel "bewitched, bothered and bewildered."

It's at these times that we should have compassion for ourselves, or for others we know who are experiencing this state, for it is a state of psychological hunger, perhaps even starvation. It is a state of psychological nutrient deprivation. It is a state that needs to be attended to with the same concern and empathy as we would attend to a state of vitamin deprivation such as scurvy.

Sometimes we feel mentally very focused and centered. Our mind is coming up with all sorts of bright ideas and seems to be clicking along keenly. At other times, we feel mentally foggy, clumsy, irritable, anxious, and a little "out of it." We may have subtle physical symptoms or pains. We feel "not quite right," "at sixes and sevens," "out of kilter," or "out of sorts." These are all colloquialisms our culture has created to describe these states of psychological hunger. And because so many such terms have been coined by our society, we know that these states are a fragment of the human experience and, therefore, deserve our attention and understanding. It is worth emphasizing again that we need the same balance of food groups no matter what age we are, and that we never outgrow *any* of the needs we have. Our needs may differ from time-to-time in their intensity (as does any need for food), but we always need balanced nutrition from each group to feel strong, vital and alive.

When I was 13 years old, I remember asking my mother who

was 39 at the time (which seemed very, very old to me), how it felt to be "that old." She, a dear, loving, and introspective woman, told me that it felt "exactly the same as it felt to be 13." My mouth dropped. I was stunned – so stunned that this conversation has stuck in my mind for 42 years now. But it is true. The self *is* constant over time. Though the self has a past, a present, and a future, people experience themselves as having essentially the same personality over time. We grow and develop, but we continue to have the same basic, elemental needs. What I have learned in my therapy practice from working with people of all ages is that during development we become aware of our needs and (hopefully) we learn to deal with them more flexibly, more creatively, and more actively. We learn to "bounce back" and be more resilient.

Dave's life illustrates, and his movies portray, that if you can learn to "eat right," you can empower yourself to bounce back when you need to. That is, if you know what the five basic Psychological Food Groups are, and also if you are alert to the symptoms that occur when your psychological needs are not being met (if you know how to recognize the signs and symptoms of hunger), you can take matters into your own hands (or fork!) and move forward. You have choices. It's your menu and a menu that only you can design. Because you are honoring your True Self, only you know what foods give you energy. The saving message here is that you do not have to wait passively for someone else to "save the day."

With the language you will learn in this chapter, you can verbalize to people who matter to you what you need. You will understand both what your child needs and what you need. This knowledge in itself raises the probability that your needs will be met. Having words to express one's needs is one of the greatest tools one can have for success. Giving a child words for his or her needs is one of the greatest gifts you can give to promote success. Through learning the words, you can help a child shape his or her environment, and you can shape your own environment. With the learning you will glean from this chapter, you will be able to assemble a menu of choices that will create a "balanced psychological diet" for healthy vitality.

In this regard, I am impressed to see that some children have exhibited the natural ability to shape their caretakers to give them the psychological nutrition they need. Through their own gifts, they have been able to "court" otherwise indifferent caretakers, or creatively to find surrogate caretakers in the neighborhood, in school, in grandparents or aunts and uncles.

The essence of what pediatrician and psychoanalyst Donald Winnicott called a "good enough mother" is similar to what a "good enough" childhood is, or even a "good enough" psychotherapist. This would be a person, or persons, who help individuals learn about themselves, define their nutritional needs, including what hungers may still be left over, in order to better negotiate needs in adult life. Having the words to describe needs from all five Psychological Food Groups is the best insurance policy one can have, both for a happy life and for the ability to bounce back. An aware and growing human being learns how joyfully to get his needs met sufficiently in the world, so he can participate in the unfolding of his True Self. In doing this, a person learns to reject environmental conditions that foist debris on his developing flower (self) and also to shape the people in his environment to feed him well. Parents must learn to recognize "a particular blossom" in their children and to provide the psychological nutrients needed in order for their child to thrive. Parents must also be equipped to help resuscitate the child's efflorescence when life's inevitable blows cause his bloom to fade, shrivel or be threatened with worse. And adults must be equipped and feel both validated and empowered to do the same thing for themselves. This is the key to being able to bounce back.

Dave and I believe that everyone has potential waiting to be activated, like a bulb lying dormant in the ground, waiting to bloom into some variety of a flower. If one is fortunate to grow up in a fertile atmosphere, naturally rich in all of the five basic Psychological Food Groups, it is more likely that this bloom will burst forth sooner and more fully, not impeded by the rubble of shame and the fear of disappointing others. If one has been raised in a more impoverished terrain, it becomes one's responsibility to recognize that and to seek out a greener pasture. The first step is having the words for the nutrients you need and giving yourself permission to compose your own menu.

Whether we happen to be blessed with enriched early childhood nourishment or not, none of us is immune from life's troubles, ordeals, and reversals – all of which deplete us of the energy and nutrients we need to "press on." Knowledge of these five basic Psychological Food Groups is our tool at these times for pulling up and out of a collapse, getting back on our feet after a hard knock, extricating ourselves from an exhausting snag or frustration, recovering from a disillusionment, pulling out of a situation of shame and guilt – and returning to the sunshine.

## CONNECTEDNESS & BELONGING

With the five Psychological Food Groups, we must first consider the bottom, most basic and most essential part of the food pyramid: the need for connectedness and belonging. Babies' need for connectedness is probably "wired in" biologically. This need has been studied by infant researchers for decades, and there is a great deal of data about how early the baby recognizes the mother's voice and fixes on the mother's eyes. This drive for connection is currently considered the most essential ingredient of being human, and all sorts of mental and physical illnesses can be documented when this innate need for connectedness is disrupted. All we have to do is witness some of the tragic stories of children abandoned in orphanages for long periods of time, without human touch, to see how drastic the effects of that lack of connection are on their later failure to thrive, to develop interpersonal relationships and to learn.

For a number of years, the Institute of Heartmath has run seminars publicizing the discovery that our heart influences brain function. Sometimes this influence has been called "emotional intelligence." The main point made is that the emotions programmed into a child's heart have a physiological effect and can change neurological pathways in the brain. The institute maintains that this heart-brain connection can influence intellectual as well as creative development and also social life.

This research also shows how important emotions are for regulating the body, the brain, memory and learning. In fact, when we are emotionally upset, so much neural action is affected that much of our learning, memory, and problem solving, are also affected. When we are anxious, fearful, or angry, the response of our brain is affected. So, helping children to develop emotional intelligence through loving connections can be as critical to survival as developing any other kind of intelligence. According to the Institute of Heartmath, positive messages of connection, if repeated over and over, can affect physiological pathways and create emotional intelligence.

In fact, the need for connectedness probably begins even before birth. William Sears, M.D., and Martha Sears are the authors of *Attachment Parenting* and the people who give some of the soundest guidance for parenting today. They say:

"Children who learn early on what it is to be connected to others and to be able to trust them try to maintain or regain this connectedness as they grow into adulthood. They follow that early blueprint and bring the trust they learned in their first relationship into later relationships. That blueprint also shows them how to trust themselves, and this self-confidence sees a child through significant adversity. Children carry the connectedness they learned as infants through the rest of their lives. It becomes a part of their overall wellbeing and makes them resilient."

*(The Successful Child*, p. 7)

Thus connectedness is the *most basic of needs* and underlies and influences all of the other human needs. Even when we are alone on that hypothetical desert island, if we are to survive psychologically, we must be in emotional connection with someone whom we know or have known and whom we experience as having loved us. This feeling of belonging is the bedrock of mental health and emotional well-being. There is fascinating contemporary research in psychoneurobiology which reflects the effect of bodily connection and touch on physical health as well as intelligence. All of the other psychological needs above on the pyramid have their basis in connection and are also aspects of connection, for they all involve a connection with other people.

One of Dave's values is continually to advance his work and achievements while keeping his personal relationships nurtured. The theme of connectedness rings through Dave's life and childhood as well as his movies. His attitude of cherishing relationships is particularly evident in the movies with Becky, in which he calls her "the best friend I could ever have" (*There Goes a Rescue Vehicle*). Despite the frustrations of their antics together, Dave and Becky always take for granted and offer their goodwill to each other. In addition, they affirm their connectedness with important others: "We can't let the team down" (*There Goes a Race Car*); "We can't let Frank down" (*There Goes a Monster Truck*). Dave frequently emphasizes the importance of independence as well: "You should never be afraid to ask for help," he says in *There Goes a Race Car*, and in virtually all his movies he says, "You should always listen to the instructor."

In Dave's personal life as well, he makes a commitment to take time for friends in what he calls his "mutual support team." Most importantly in his marriage now to Rebecca, he has integrated both love and work. Rebecca is a beautiful, soft-spoken, feminine, and very competent woman, who combines many types of connections: she is Dave's wife, lover, business partner, expert consultant for his business, and the mother of the four children they are raising together.

Always looking at his work and world as a "playground," Dave's movies reflect the exuberance of connection with one's inner child. In *There Goes a Roller Coaster*, Dave's "son" reintroduces him to roller coaster rides at a huge amusement park and experiences immense pleasure when Dave can fully regress to his own childhood – the days when eating junk food, riding rides, meeting Bugs Bunny, petting farm animals, balancing on a curb and trying on funny hats were the high point of life.

Psychoanalysts have long known that the capacity to play is the basis of early connectedness and gives children a bedrock of self-confidence and security. From very early on, messages of acceptance and lovableness are communicated through physical play, through touch and skin contact. And research now shows that stimulation to the skin sends messages to the brain that affects its development. Researchers such as Harry Harlow and Tiffany Field, a developmental psychologist, are famous for linking touch and attachment. And in her book called *Baby Massage* Tiffany Field describes how touch enhances the parent-child bond. In her more academic research, she has found that touch appears to be an important neurological and immune system regulator for all of us.

Other researchers have also shown that connectedness through touch is essential for children's neurological and emotional development. And it has also been recognized that if the elderly do not receive enough touch, they can develop both physical and psychological problems that can also affect their learning.

A stunning psychological experiment first drew attention to the connection between touch and learning. The experiment was designed to measure the ability of different rats to accomplish certain cognitive or learning tasks. The psychologists were surprised and puzzled to find that the rats that were kept on the upper cages in the lab room were scoring markedly higher on their "intellectual" performances than the rats that were living in the lower cages in the lab. Statistically, of course, this was totally improbable, if not impossible! And so, the psychologists were challenged to come up with an explanation. The only explanation which could describe this difference was that the rats in the upper cages had to be picked up by hand and *held* during their feedings several times a day, while those in the bottom cages could just have their food tossed into their cages. The psychologists were amazed that this small amount of touch and holding, even with rodents, could dramatically affect their ability to learn. Just think what it can do for human babies. Pediatricians William and Martha Sears have written a series of wonderful books for parents based on their deep understanding of the need for holding, touch and connectedness as the bedrock for all of childhood development. I heartily recommend these books for all parents. This early connection with caretakers builds good feelings and fosters a sense of internal wellbeing. As Dominican friar Sam

Mattarazzo maintains, "The key to independence is successful dependence."

Dave's personal style as well as his movie persona demonstrates the ready arm around a friend's back, the ready hug of appreciation, the warm communication, even without language, that "you belong with me, kids." There are now New York City-based peer play groups that teach children the social and emotional skills to help them overcome the pain and shame of feeling "left out." The founders, Andrew Cohen and Sander Greenbaum, assert that the biggest advantage that such groups can offer is the sense of belonging and being accepted.

In Dave's movies, he transmits this welcoming feeling right across the air, and meeting him in person gives exactly the same impression. He exudes play, warmth… a "psychological embrace." Even Dave's phrase, "I'm ready if you're ready," gives the feeling of mutuality, togetherness, or belonging. These movies are, at base, all about emotional support. None of the characters rejects or degrades another. I am convinced that this subliminal message of emotional support is one of the reasons that the movies are so popular; they are soothing to viewers. In fact, one patient of mine (age 48), to whom I gave one of Dave's movies in hopes that it would help heal his feelings of shame, told me that it helped him so much the package should not say, "Ages 3-8," but rather "For all ages."

As the Searses advocate and as Dave and I strongly maintain, if one has had a feeling of connectedness and belonging with early caretakers from the beginning of life, one has a distinct advantage. So often, when we are down or depressed, we withdraw. Our connection with others is the first thing we relinquish or let go of. The moral of the story is that we need to resist the pull to seclude ourselves. In a landmark UCLA study, psychologists Taylor, Klein, Lewis, Gruenewald, Gurung, and Updegraff, showed fascinating gender differences in this regard. While males tend to use fight or flight as a behavioral response to stress, women have a larger behavioral repertoire and they're more likely to "tend and befriend." The authors go on to say that this may be why women consistently outlive men, since study after study has found that social ties reduce our risk of disease by lowering blood pressure, heart rate, and cholesterol.

As a corollary, we need to use what has been learned about tending and befriending to help others who seem depleted or depressed, whether they are aware of it or not. Many studies have shown that people who are deprived of friends are at greater risk for premature death, and that lack of companionship is more dangerous to survival than smoking. There is a famous Nurses Health Study from Harvard Medical School that found that the more friends women had, the less likely they were to develop physical ailments as they aged. So, it is a terrible mistake to put our friends on the back burner when they can add years to our lives – not to mention quality and enjoyment.

Still other studies show that elderly people who had heart attacks were more likely to die in the hospital if no one visited them. Even if they receive only one visitor their life span increased and continued to increase as visitors came (Luskin, p. 41). Research has also shown that having supportive family and friends can even help prevent us from getting sick in the first place. A priest friend of mine whose good council I have come to rely upon summed it up when he said, "Just living requires group support." (Dominican friar Sam Mattarazzo) Without group support, the immune system can be suppressed, often leading to a cold or a worse ailment (Dodes p. 82). David Siegel, M.D., whom I knew from early in my training in the 1970s at the Massachusetts Mental Health Center in Boston, has done groundbreaking research which has documented that women with advanced metastatic breast cancer live longer, by at least five years, if they participate in breast cancer support groups.

Dave's movies' ooze feelings of support. They show happy, warm and positive relations between people. I think that viewers are both consciously and subconsciously drawn to this. I think that is what happened with Grant and me during those hundreds of hours that we watched Dave's movies – long before I started *consciously thinking* about "what is going on here?"

Take out your blank pyramid worksheet now and fill in the people, places, things or activities that give you feelings of safety, connection, acceptance, warmth, support, physical or psychological "hugs," belonging – or, as a patient of mine once called it, "warm fuzzies."

The guiding principle for this goal of development is never really separation as was promoted by many psychologists in the '60s, or renouncing the need for "dependence" on other people. Rather, the goal is to find ways to keep connected with people whom we *can depend on* for the nourishment we need and who can depend on us for the same. This is crucial whether we are first realizing our dreams or bouncing back to our dreams after a setback.

# MIRRORING & AFFIRMATION

The next need in the Psychological Nutrition Pyramid also begins very early in life. This is the need for mirroring and affirmation. Metaphorically, mirroring is when someone else holds up a mirror to you, so to speak, enabling you to see yourself. This can be noticing something personal about you, noticing something about your looks, your being, your specialness, your uniqueness, or something that you have done or accomplished

In infancy, mirroring can be seen most dramatically when a mother cradles her baby and gazes into his eyes, transmitting the message (either verbally or just through the expression on her face), "Mommy loves you;" "You are the most wondrous, most perfect and magnificent child in the whole world!" This sparkle in the mother's eye, the "look of love," the gaze of admiration, awe, adoration and enchantment, reflects pride, and exudes a feeling of specialness which is shared by both mother and child alike. Psychoanalyst Heinz Kohut defined the word special as meaning, unique, valued and important, non-exalted or grandiose.

Again, our culture is aware of the significance of this emotional experience. We have colloquial expressions such as "the gleam in the mother's eye," "the apple of her eye," and "I only have eyes for you," and when this affirming mirroring is in place, a basic bedrock of positive self-esteem begins to solidify. The roots of a strong and self-confident individual begin to sprout and to grow. Philip Moffitt calls this "nurturing with joy." It celebrates the existence of the child as a source of delight for the one who is mothering. The joyful feeling shows in mother and child and continues in the child into adulthood as a sense of innate worth and spontaneity.

On the other hand, should the mother happen to be depressed, or if her eyes are for some reason "dead and gleamless," the child will come to feel, very early on, even before there are words to describe this experience, that he is "nothing special." Patients who come to me convinced that they are boring, not inspiring, or that there is nothing interesting or special about them, often, upon exploration of their history, can be found to have had mothers or caretakers who, for one reason or another, had been chronically unable to give them this sort of mirroring. They may have been good at providing for the child's basic needs but they were unable to make their child feel treasured and cherished. An exhausted parent may be too tired to become excited about her child. Her face may be blank, not out of ill will, but out of her own depletion and exhaustion. She therefore may not be able to kindle a child's feeling of being special or interesting or exciting himself. A mother who has lost a parent may be deeply depressed and disheartened and be unable to attend fully to or invest in her child emotionally. The child then gleans the feeling that "there is no joy to be gotten from me" or "there is no tangible pleasure to be gotten from me." These early beliefs and feelings linger beneath the surface, out of full conscious awareness, often until they are brought forth and put into words through talking with a close friend or in therapy. In the meantime, this sort of child may compensate for their feelings by trying to become extra wonderful, inexhaustibly entertaining, maybe even a child prodigy, in order to get the mirroring or excitement that is his birthright. Hollywood is filled with such cases – children deprived early on of mirroring who use their talents compulsively to get attention, and who, sadly, can never be satisfied with all the applause or accolades they receive. These are the same people who frequently collapse emotionally, or turn to drugs and alcohol, when their days of splendor on the stage run out and they have to face the pain of their internal unmirrored childhood self.

Sometimes people who are convinced that they are not special do the opposite of becoming entertaining and exhibitionistic. They "shrink into the woodwork." They are pulled to remain "backstage," an expression Irving Goffman coined in his book *The Presentation of Self in Everyday Life* (1972). These individuals consistently shrink from self-presentation and visibility because of a depleted sense of vitality and self-worth. And there is also a third alternative for the unmirrored self: these are the individuals who do not become exhibitionistic and seek applause, nor do they shrink into the woodwork out of a depleted sense of vitality. These people live out rather "normal"- appearing lives but live in a state of depression and boredom. The reason for this is that they cannot "process" or "take in" any input that could be experienced as mirroring. That is, because they have such a strong conviction that they are not special, if they are invited to a social occasion, given a compliment, or told that they are liked or loved these compliments or "good vibes" have nothing to stick to. I often say to patients such as this, "You have no storage file on your computer for such input." Because the lack of mirroring goes so far back in their childhood and their belief that there is "no joy to be had" from them, anything positive literally "goes in one ear and out the other."

As with all of the other nutritional food groups, our need for mirroring is central to infancy and early childhood, but we never outgrow it. Babies need to be noticed, "ooohed and aaahed" over, to be seen and paid attention to. As adults, we need mirroring as well. As we mature, hopefully we don't only need to hear "oh, aren't you beautiful, aren't you wonderful." But we might need to hear that from time to time from our significant other (or our mother). But through growth and maturation we should be able to develop flexibility in being able to get attention, appreciation or praise more indirectly. We might get it from being accepted to a first-choice college or by getting a compliment from a teacher or boss or by having a book accepted for publication. An invitation to a party can provide a mirroring experience.

For some reason, Dave's family instinctively knew a lot about mirroring. His mother said, "I remember when the children were very small and they would see their father coming home; they would gather at the door and say, 'We love you, Dad!'" And human nature is such that when people receive this kind of positive mirroring, they usually give it back. Dave and his sister both heard a lot of "I love you too." Light from mirrors reflects and refracts, as Dave likes to say, "The light you shine on someone else often shines back on you."

Even when we are not getting direct mirroring from the outside, we can learn to use our experience to generate a feeling of mirroring from within ourselves. We can do this by remembering times when we have gotten admiration, by looking back and recalling messages of feeling wanted, appreciated, or complimented. For example, an actor in my practice has been out of work for several months now, but he is able not to lose heart because he remembers how popular his last performances were and the wonderful reviews he had in the newspapers. These memories have kept his spirits buoyed up despite his current empty schedule.

Children are very susceptible to a lack of mirroring because it is the second most basic need of the Psychological Nutrition Pyramid. They crave this food and it is much needed if they are to thrive. Because they are so young and undeveloped, they need the most affirmation to know who they are and what about them is valuable. If, in growing up, children are deprived of this, if their mothers were "flat faced," and were unable to give them a feeling of specialness (mirroring) or of being cherished, they will grow up to be adults who are excessively vulnerable to a lack of these kinds of mirroring responses in their environment. They will become what our culture calls "thin-skinned"; "having a chip on his shoulder"; "touchy or easily injured." An example comes from the movie *Avalon*. Do you remember the oldest brother who was so injured when he was very late for Thanksgiving dinner and the family did not wait for him to begin carving the turkey that he did not speak to members of his family for decades? This is an excellent example of an adult who is excessively vulnerable to a slight or a lack of a mirroring response in the environment. Virtually in all such adults one can find a history of deprivation, of mirroring in early childhood that leaves them with such vulnerability.

One patient of mine is constantly tense because she finds herself scanning her work world at all times, looking into the eyes of her co-workers for signs of whether they "like me" or "don't." Every time her boss puts red marks on her writing she gets very upset and experiences this "criticism" as devastating. It totally, for that day, erases her sense of value. My patient had grown up with a depressed mother, overburdened with seven older siblings, who was unable to give her the attention and validation that she needed. In addition, her older siblings were always putting her down, calling her "the baby," even when she was in her 20s and, now that she is in her 40s, they continue to ridicule and devalue any ideas and plans that she has, treating her as if both her brain and her character are still infantile.

In contrast, another patient of mine travels worldwide giving speeches for a pharmaceutical company on topics that could be considered rather dry. Frequently, people at these training seminars nod off and fall asleep or actually walk out in the midst of the presentation. While a more vulnerable presenter might feel hurt or discouraged by such a visible lack of attentiveness, my patient doesn't take this lack of attentiveness personally. He attributes the un-interest to the dryness of the material and not to himself as boring. He even has empathy for the people who are required to attend his long presentations.

This patient was raised by a mother and father who adored him, two older sisters who were devoted to him, and two sets of attentive grandparents who lived nearby. For him, the lower part of his food pyramid was "filled up," and he had plenty to draw on within his own mind when he was not getting enough mirroring in his current life. It is not that he had no reaction to the lack of mirroring. Of course he was disappointed because he spent long hours preparing PowerPoint presentations, but he was able to talk to himself and re-equilibrate and remember the times that he had been given good feelings about himself as an interesting person and speaker. The lack of mirroring in the current day did not activate a prior negative self-image telling him that there was nothing interesting about him. Because he could rely on earlier positive experiences of feeling admired and appreciated (which he had stored in his own "computer file," in his mind) he could let these hurts roll off his back like water off a duck.

The main difference between being young and being older is that when you are older, you have more experience to draw on, so that you can remember positive past experiences; you know what you need; and you have the flexibility to find other places to get the kind of nourishment you need. The patient who gave pharmaceutical talks also had a group of colleagues who accompanied him to his lectures, so he could always look forward to delicious dinners in fancy restaurants with a lot of collegial conviviality at the end of his long presentations. He also knew that he could go back to the hotel room, take a shower, work out in the health club, and call his wife and children for a loving response. So he knew where to get the mirroring responses he needed to keep him feeling good.

The central point is that as people mature, they do not outgrow their needs for mirroring but they develop a broader menu of places to go to get these nutritional needs met. If a friend of mine is walking down the street and does not acknowledge me, of course I will feel a little hurt, disturbed and out of balance, because I will have been deprived of the acknowledgment or mirroring I need. As the kids say, "I will have been dissed!" But, hopefully I will have had enough experience with friends who do acknowledge me, or who have acknowledged me in the past, that I will either be able to remind myself of these, or I will be able to go about finding at least one other friend that day (or the next day) who will react positively to me.

It is crucial for parents to recognize the need for mirroring and to acknowledge how basic it is to our "food chain," both for our children and for ourselves. We need to validate the fact that people need to be affirmed, remembered, and recognized. We all need this at every phase of life. Interview your children to find out who they are. Providing listening and understanding is probably the most basic form of mirroring a person can give. Just feeling heard and understood without being interrupted provides a nest egg of self-worth for a child. Knowing this fact, then, have you ever thought how ironic it is for our society that, as soon as a child starts to learn to talk we tell him to "be quiet."

The same holds true for adults. It only takes one person to open new blossoms of the self that are nascent within all of us and to enable them to grow and develop so that we can reach our innate potential. The act of listening and affirmation provides the fertilizer that feeds the sprouting flower. As with a plant (or a rocket, or a car), it has to be fed good food. If you want it to "shoot up," you have to put *good* fuel in. Who knows what wondrous blossoms are in there ready to germinate? And beware: never, never convey the message that there is something wrong with a bud, or a leaf, or a stem, or a root, if you want your plant to keep lifting upwards and be strong.

Psychotherapists Cynthia Feigel and Howard Glasser teach parents about an approach to parenting which focuses on the conscious use of mirroring. They call it "The Nurtured Heart" approach. They advocate being alert to your child's tiny successes and focusing big energy and appreciation on the successes (mirroring them) in order to build a positive sense of self. Dr. Feigel advises, "Let your children hear you brag about them or overhear you doing it." "Build your child up in every area of their life; let them know they are a success and that they *can do* things." "Tell a child the *next day* that you remember their success, because if you hold their success in your heart, and remember it, it causes a major physiological response." "Give them intense, heartfelt appreciation and pride and amazement for the good things that they do." Mirroring is so powerful that Feigel and Glasser believe that if you mirror the behaviors you want from the child, the child will repeat them, spontaneously letting go of un-mirrored behaviors (behaviors you don't want).

Research is showing that positive messages actually build neuropathways in the brain that build in a belief that one is a success and someone who can accomplish things. Children's literature has known this all along (note the publication in 1955 of *Scuffy the Tug Boat*) but now science is establishing this fact medically. The whole field of Heart Math, which can be accessed on the Web site www. heartmath.com, shows that positive input creates a physiological response in the heart that programs the brain. If we give them our "radical amazement" (a phrase from Abraham J. Heschel) then it seems we are able to program a success attitude in our children.

Such appreciation, if shared out loud with emotional intensity, shapes successes and mirrors positive self-esteem. It is the nourishment that creates a solid base on which a healthy sense of self can grow. It is very much like the sport of curling. We are using our enthusiasm to facilitate movement much like the broom energetically sweeps the way in front of the stone to clear its course. But here, we are helping sweep forward someone's own natural trajectory.

As adults, at some times during our lives this nutritional need for mirroring is more in the foreground than at other times. In general, it's at the times when we are pressing the envelope of growth into new areas that we need more mirroring. Once when I was trying to do a new creative project that was outside my field of expertise, I called my husband on the phone every couple of hours to read him sections of the manuscript, since the topic was so new to me, and I felt so unsure of myself. I would call and announce: "I have written four pages and I need some mirroring!" We would giggle together and he would listen, very conscious of the validity of my need to have my efforts appreciated. Sometimes, my actual production wasn't really all that great. All I needed at those times was the affirmation that I was working hard, making progress or sustaining my effort despite discouragement. Sometimes all the mirroring people need is to be told that they should take pride in having put forth their best efforts for a cause they deeply value (a goal of their "True Self") even if the actual goal cannot be reached.

Dave's history is noteworthy in that he was blessed with a mother and father who gave him active and vigorous mirroring. They cheered him on in his endeavors and encouraged him to believe in his abilities and in his worth. They clapped for his many dramatic performances at home and at school, laughed at his jokes, and told him he had great potential and that he could become anything he wanted to become. My interviews with Dave, his sister, and his parents all concurred that the guidance Dave received was "gentle," and that the family's response to his enthusiasm was always positively tinged.

Perhaps Dave's personal history of warmth and mirroring is why his movies are so naturally replete with so many models of healthy mirroring. When you watch them, it is intriguing to see the relationship between Dave and Becky and how happy and mutually supportive their interaction is (which enables these sometimes harrowing adventures to proceed so pleasingly and successfully). In *There Goes a Motorcycle*, Dave says to Becky (who finally finds becoming motorcycle gear after many attempts to select a suit that looks good on her), "You look good. You look so good you're fogging up my goggles!" Another example is in *There Goes a Train*. The conductor says to Dave (after a close call where they nearly collided with a car stuck on the railroad tracks), "Thanks Engineer Dave, you saved the day!" In a surprise turnaround, monster truck driving teacher Frank finds a way to rescue Dave's self-esteem after he has run over his father's car while learning to drive a monster truck when he says, "Good job, Dave. I couldn't have done better." In *There Goes a Rescue Vehicle*, Dave tumbles head over heels over a cliff and has to be pulled out of the bushes in a gurney (because Becky had thrown him off balance by blowing the horn in the truck). They bicker for 30 seconds; then Dave apologizes for scolding her and says that she's the "best friend a person could ever have." Talk about mirroring!

The Dave movies offer a consistent model for helping to raise successful children with the enthusiastic use of mirroring. For example, when a child is trying something new, you mirror him for the effort. If you say, "What makes you think you can do this when people smarter than you can't do it?" you crush the child's developing potential. You crush his desire to explore his abilities. You crush his bud. You would be surprised at how many parents respond this way to their children. "Negative attention is life's emotional junk food, it has no nutritional value. Although not intended that way, it makes children weaker on the inside and downloads as failure." (Cynthia Feigel) If you deprive your child of mirroring, however unconsciously, you withhold the nutrient he needs to pursue success; you withhold the response he needs to be inspired to continue to learn and to feel confident. A Charlie Brown cartoon that I've seen shows Lucy yelling all sorts of insults at Charlie Brown, then innocently looking at him and asking, "Why aren't you singing?"

Shaming a child, or using words that relate to the "language of shame" (Morrison) such as calling him foolish, stupid, dumb, or inadequate, will only cause aggression, shyness, or the withering of potential. Enlightened child psychologists have ceased using the phrase "difficult child" and now refer to the "spirited child" (*Raising Your Spirited Child*, Mary Sheedy Kurcinka, 1998). There is a "translation list" to help parents who are frustrated by the pressures of daily living to reframe their child's behaviors to foster a positive self-image. For example "whiney" is translated to "expressive," "bossy" to "future manager," "demanding" to "persistent." Besides never calling names, a guideline also seen in the Dave movies is that no one is ever cynical. Cynicism is just veiled anger, which is a sure-fire method to lower self-esteem and cause the wilting or twisting of the flower. Despite this knowledge it may be difficult for a parent positively to mirror a child and to refrain from using shaming words if this approach differs greatly from the way they, themselves, were raised. If this is the case, talking with a friend, spouse, or counselor is of great importance considering how basic the need for mirroring is for a happy, healthy and productive life.

As adults, knowing where to get the food supply of mirroring is crucial if we are to successfully bounce back from a calamity, a life blow, a slip or a fall – or if we are going to be able to recover from one of life's hard knocks. Again, the first step is validating for ourselves the need for mirroring. This is especially important if mirroring has not been a large part of our own childhood nutrition. It is important to not be shy or embarrassed about admitting to one's self that mirroring is an important psychological nutritional need – not just in childhood, but through all the life cycle. When we show symptoms of depletion, depression, shame or low self-esteem, finding places where we can get appreciation, admiration, and even love, can give us the "shot in the arm" that will enable us to move on to the next day and, eventually, back on track towards our dreams. This is especially true when we have experienced loss, sorrow or shame experiences, or life experiences in which our self-esteem has been battered, or we have been left feeling battered, bedraggled, beaten down, bruised or befuddled.

In summary, the strong emphasis on mirroring and affirmation in the Dave movies illustrates that we all need these types of nutrition from our interpersonal environment in order to help us flourish into our true potential. Getting these nutritional needs met can mean the difference between bursting forth and actually doing something that has seemed like only a dream or being able to resuscitate a dream that has been crushed. Just as we all need oxygen from the atmosphere, so do we need responses from our interpersonal environment in order to thrive, develop our True Self, or restore a self that has been squished.

Take some time now to fill in the "mirroring" portion of your pyramid with the people and places you could go to for admiration, validation, or simply a pat on the back. As with any of the five psychological nutritional needs, if you can't think of anyone or any place in your present environment, it's time to start to think about expanding your environment and finding another garden. By now you should have well internalized the point that you cannot deny your psychological nutritional needs any more than you can deny your biological need for food.

# IDEALIZATION & HEROES

The next step up on the Psychological Nutrition Pyramid – and another need that we never outgrow – is the need for idealization and heroes. Idealization is the need to feel connected to someone whom we can look up to, admire, and thereby feel an enhanced sense of power and importance. With idealization comes the feeling of being taken care of and protected.

A child develops by moving along from the enjoyment of being primarily the "gleam in his mother's eye" to having an increased longing to be near someone big and powerful, someone he can idealize. An idealizable figure can be anyone who can be looked up to whom the child can feel close to and gain a sense of strength from, sort of by "proxy," as if his power could "rub off." Often, in families, this figure is the father, but not necessarily. The key is that if idealization is working right the child feels enhanced by his relationship with the idealized figure, not diminished by it.

As with the other nutritional needs, this need to idealize starts in childhood. But throughout our entire lives, we all need to have people to admire and to feel enhanced and protected through being connected with them. In early childhood, the image that comes to mind is that of a little boy standing at the sink with his father, pretending to shave his face with a bladeless razor and daubs of shaving cream. For these precious moments, the child pictures himself as being grown up, just like his father. When my 4-year-old son enacts this with his dad, he often pictures himself being so grown up that he imagines that he really does have a beard, and he frequently asks me to come and feel how smooth his face is now! Little girls might stand side by side with their mothers as dinner is prepared for the family, proudly showing off the finished product saying, "and I helped!" (as in the old ad for Shake 'n Bake). Once again, our society intuitively recognizes these needs by having colloquial expressions such as "chip off the old block," or "the apple doesn't fall far from the tree."

As children grow, they are lucky if there are idealizable figures for them to be close to in their immediate environment. These can be parents, aunts and uncles, coaches, teachers, or various other mentors. During childhood, this need for heroes is often expressed in a global way, such as "my father can beat up your father" or "my father is a policeman," or in the new television ad, "My father owns Nike!" (which is amusing to viewers when they see an average-looking dad coming on to the scene with the text on the screen, "owns two shares." Some of Dave's early heroes were, his father, grandfather, Red Skelton, Rod Serling, Jimmy Stewart, John Wayne, and Walt Disney.

As people mature, the need is less to idealize the whole person than to admire and idealize aspects or characteristics of someone. Adults might have political figures whose ideologies they respect or religious organizations whose theology appeals to them. Most senior psychoanalysts have respected colleagues to consult. Although I have been in practice for 30 years, I know very well the boost of self-esteem and sense of vitalization that I get in being associated with international experts in my field and being able to call upon their experience when I need help in a particularly challenging clinical situation.

Often, if we are lucky we idealize our doctors whom we see as protecting us. A good example is my father, who is a long-term survivor of prostate cancer – 10 years now and hopefully well into the future. He happens to see an extremely compassionate, empathic, and wise doctor who, although he is significantly *younger* than my father, offers my father a wonderful example of idealization from which Dad gains great comfort.

The other day, when Dad received a PSA reading that was worrisome, Dr. Sufrin said to him, "Don't you worry about that. Leave the worrying to *me*. I'll take care of you, so trust me; go along on your way and I'll figure out what we'll do by the time I see you next month." This wonderful example shows that one does not have to be older to be an idealizable figure, but one does have to be empathic. The strength and protectiveness of Dr. Sufrin relieved the anxiety of my father, and of all the members of my family, including my brother who also happens to be a doctor.

As we proceed through life, our idealizations can be more abstract, such as theories or philosophies that we hold dear or which give us a feeling of direction and strength. For example, Dave and I could be said to idealize the concept of resilience and the idea that people can bounce back from a "shouldn't have done that." In working together, we found that we both draw strength from our belief in the **P.R.I.D.E. Factor**™ and how it, along with the Psychological Nutrition Pyramid, allows people to find the resources they need to bounce back from life's inevitable setbacks. It can be said then that this healthy idealization is what brought Dave and me together in the first place and inspired us to write this guide together.

Dave's own personal life and history, as well as the stories from the movies, are replete with many grown-up figures who are idealizable to children: firefighters, police officers, pilots, astronauts, train engineers, ship captains, rescue heroes, and military personnel. Importantly, all of them enthusiastically express the feeling that theirs is the "best job in the world," and that any kid can have that job if he stays in school and keeps studying. The presence of an admired figure, combined with the possibility of the child's approaching that person's stature, is a big nutritional supplement for a growing child with a motivation to succeed.

This point is extremely important. The child must feel that he, too, has the potential to reach the stature of the figure whom he idealizes. If the hero is too far up on a pedestal and the child is given no hope of ever being able to become "that great" *himself*, the child will not be inspired to try to stretch and grow. A patient of mine described a motivating idealization situation perfectly: "I knew I wanted to become a priest when I saw the assistant priest standing on a ladder in his T-shirt painting the walls of the auditorium. He is a far cry from the actual pastor who is the old-fashioned 'king of the hill.' Father Al was a regular guy who could wield a paintbrush, whom I could look up to, but he was not unreachable. His pedestal was his paint ladder." In all of the Dave movies, the emphasis is on how *you too can become* an astronaut, etc., if you just stay in school and study.

Dave likes to quote Sophocles: "Would it be, I admit, that men should be right by instinct, but since we are likely to go astray, the reasonable thing is to learn from those who can teach." Dave has, in his own life, surrounded himself with teachers (idealization figures). He has made it a habit to observe others, to study public figures and affirm what they do well, what makes them different, and also what attracts people to them. Intuitively, he always looked to wise, older people for guidance. He made a habit of reading success stories of people he admired, and studied their "winning methods." He watched television movies and shows and selected characters whom he could visualize as heroes. He oriented himself to following the stories of "winners," and he advocates the importance of finding someone you respect, who has admirable characteristics, and imagining yourself handling problems as that person would handle them.

Dave was lucky in that his own father offered him sage guidance and advice, but it was Dave's grandfather who, as Dave's mother confirmed for me, was his first "hero" and thus one of the most dominant influences in his life. According to Dave, his grandfather "knew who he was" and what sort of work provided him with true personal contentment. Dave's grandfather guided him to find work that would make him happy. He encouraged Dave to devote his time, energy and attention to something he really loved.

Dave's grandfather was always interested in promoting Dave's development. In his grandfather's presence, Dave enjoyed the feeling of trust, safety and a sense of mutual admiration. In Dave's own words, "Anytime I went into his house, I knew I could find him in his tool-and-machine-filled basement. He seemed to have tools for making or fixing anything! I know that working alongside him, watching and listening to him, did as much for me and for my outlook and insight as anything in my life.

"He liked his job and made a comfortable living. In fact, when he was offered a promotion that would provide more money and prestige, but siphon away his time and attention from his family, he actually turned it down. He preferred a life which had a better balance between his home and his work. Much of my belief in life's meaning came from the example of my grandfather. I draw upon that positive memory of my relationship with him when I am faced with a crisis in or turning point in my own life."

It's interesting that when Dave was considering moving from radio (in which he had worked since the young age of 18) to the television and film industry, he applied his grandfather's ideals of devoting his energy to work that he loved. Once he discerned that television was his love, he made a point of meeting and talking to people in the television industry, both to experience them and to emulate them. One of these people was Charlton Heston, whose stature, discipline, grace, initiative, endurance, self-confidence, and personal ability to regulate his time and energy were qualities Dave admired and ultimately integrated into his own persona.

As mentioned earlier, the privilege of being able to feel close to a "great" person can enhance self-esteem even by proxy. Dave told me that he had noticed this phenomenon during production on a story he produced when he slept in the same bedroom in which movie giants like Clark Gable, Jean Harlow, Robert DeNiro, and Diane Keaton had stayed at the famous Chateau Marmont in Los Angeles. I knew exactly what he meant: I had had the same feeling when I was fortunate enough to have the opportunity to actually sleep in the White House!

This need for Idealization never goes away. Despite Dave's great success now, he still gets a thrill out of being with people who are well-known, capable, and creative. Dave is humble enough to appreciate that we can all be enhanced by being close to the intellectual, spiritual and emotional richness of others who have qualities of excellence we can admire.

The truth is that Dave has been fortunate enough to have had a healthy diet of idealization figures all his life, and now he has *become* one. About 10 years ago, he wrote a letter to himself that said, "Recently, I spent some time with Charlton Heston. I hope that, one day, some kid may write a letter to himself that says, 'I spent the day with Dave Hood!'" And this dream of Dave's has come true. Recently, I was with Dave when he was performing his stage show in Providence, R.I., and a little boy was overheard telling his dad, "Wow! This was the best day I've ever had in my whole life!"

In most of the success stories we hear about, one can find in the person's history an admired adult the child has looked up to. If that adult can model the way a child might turn out to be, it's like kindling a pilot light on his dreams. Children, like Dave, who are lucky also receive direct guidance and encouragement from such figures. Merely by surrounding one's self with others who have attitudes of success – people one can idealize – can give a jump-start to hope.

The theme of hope resonates in all of Dave's movies. The stories are all based on teaching children how to both respect and use teachers. Instructors are portrayed as kind and happy people who love their jobs and who know a great deal about various large vehicles. Dave's movies invite children to at least imagine emulating idealizable figures or picturing what it might be like to actually grow up and do the big things that these instructors can do.

Implicit in all of Dave's movies is the advice to "go to the experts." Remember awesome Frank, in *There Goes a Monster Truck*? And Ivan "Iron Man" Stuart, who won the Baja six times in a row in *There Goes a Race Car*? Dave knows, intuitively, that it is this capacity for idealization that enables children to *dream big* and sets children up for a sense of accomplishment and **P.R.I.D.E.**™ Children learn about real firefighters, whom they look up to, and about the details of their day-to-day lives; they learn respect for daunting vehicles like bulldozers that have to be handled with care; they learn respect for the knowledge of the conductors who drive trains; and they learn how much really goes into the skills behind being able to serve food on a moving dining car on a train, as well as how much really has to be mastered about different flags if you want to drive a race car.

In all the movies, the instructors give Dave grown-up tasks. And giving kids group tasks to do is a technique that always makes children feel "bigger." It builds a sense of "I can" that ultimately gets generalized to other new tasks and challenges. Dave himself in his movies models a kid mastering "big things." Even the feat of driving a monster truck or handling a huge bulldozer can be seen as an idealization experience because he is, by definition, becoming close to a force (although not human) much greater than himself.

Both in his *Real Wheels Live* show, and in his movies, these vehicles, although far from being flesh-and-blood human, can actually seem alive and animated. They even sometimes play tricks on Dave. They are big and strong, and the interplay with Dave conveys that "It's safe, Dave. Stay close to me; pay attention; and you can be big and strong too." Some vehicles pull, some dump, some move things, some help people rescue others, some put out fires, some lug freight, but with all, the message is always benign. It's as if Dave and his vehicles are saying, "Come out. It's OK. Everyone can become big and strong and do something big." It is pretty much guaranteed (as is conveyed many times in each video) that if you listen to the instructor, stay in school and study, you'll be able to do the same amazing thing too. What a message of hope and confidence! (I'll tell you a secret: Dave told me himself that although he's all grown up now, when he drives these big vehicles, sometimes he, himself, feels like "Mister Big.")

Now, even "Mister Big" Dave realizes that feeling big or keeping that feeling is not always easy. It can be intimidating to be up close to such awesome people or vehicles. One can see Dave work out this issue in *There Goes a Monster Truck*, where his mind is boggled that he's actually meeting Frank, the *most famous* monster truck driver in the world. Dave hesitates a bit and then moves forward – showing kids (and adults too) that they can master these natural feelings of shyness. In his live stage show, he does the same thing. He hesitates a little behind the curtain, then shows kids that they can burst forth through their shyness and end up getting the applause that they need to continue on!

Our message is that it is important for parents to recognize their children's need for idealization and to allow it to develop. I once heard a story of a little boy who was watching his father fix some plumbing under the kitchen sink. He eagerly approached his father and asked, "Dad, can I help? Can I hold your wrench? I could hold your tool box while you're fixing the drip under the sink!" The father, feeling irritable and overwrought that day, shooed his son away and said, "I don't know anything. I'm just winging it. I don't know beans about plumbing. Get away from me. I'm a flunky, and I don't know what I'm doing either."

What a crushing blow this must have been for the little boy and what a clear example of the stressed father depriving his son of his need for idealization. Did the father not know how important this nutritional need was for his son? Was the father's own self-esteem so low that he was uncomfortable with his own son's idealization? Did the father himself not have a father whom he could idealize (and gain strength from) and so not have a model for what his son needed from him? Certainly, if this becomes the pattern of the father-son relationship, the son will find it much more difficult to consolidate his self-esteem because he will be missing this basic nutrient – at least from his father. Hopefully, he will be able to find other figures both whom he can idealize, and who do not push away these feelings.

By contrast, consider a little girl who watches her father, who is an ophthalmologist, and says, "Daddy, can I watch you at work? You look through those lenses and you see *eyes*. You see what they can do. You fit glasses. That's really amazing! Can I come see what you do?" And Dad says, "Sure, come on along. You can't really do what I do with the patient, but you can help clean the glasses for me, and you can turn off the lights in the examination room and turn them on again when I tell you. That would be a great help to me."

Now, that's a great example of idealization going well. Good food! The father welcomes his daughter's idealization. And by allowing her to look up to him, he fosters her budding confidence that she could help him – she *could do something big*. Roots would be laid down for her wanting to study and her budding sense of success would be nourished. She may not say it out loud, but we could imagine that what might be going through her mind might be, "Wow, Dad's a pretty big guy who knows a lot and he's letting *me* help and making me feel really important. I can turn off the lights; I can clean the glasses, and I'm really helping and maybe someday I can be a doctor or a nurse and help people too."

Another example of the need for a powerful, idealized figure in order to enhance one's feeling of strength during times of vulnerability occurred recently with my 4-year-old son. When my husband and I took him to a social gathering in a new city, with many unfamiliar adults and children, he looked at first a little shy and unsure in the midst of all the activity and commotion. One child, about two years younger than my son, had been pursuing him with fervor, arduously trying to hug him at every chance! This assertive pursuit by a stranger made Grant feel a little overwhelmed, so he dashed off to change his clothes. Off came the cute, "preppy" navy blue and white striped shirt I had so carefully dressed him in, and on went the T-shirt we had bought that day at the Chicago Aquarium with faces of huge sharks, all with their mouths open in frightening images. Wearing his new shirt, Grant felt empowered to take on the crowd and mix with strangers. What a perfect example of merging with (to Grant's eye) a powerful and "idealizable" figure – a shark!

Another example also involves my son. Though he potty-trained himself at 9 months, he still sometimes has accidents during the night while he sleeps. So, he wears a pull-up diaper just to be sure. For a long time he treasured the Sesame Street diaper with Ernie, Grover and Big Bird on the front. But one night he emphatically declared to me, "Mom, take these off! I want the 'diap' that has Buzz Lightyear. He's a *hero*!" Obviously Grant was struggling with the vulnerability of still once in a while being unable to make it through the night without wetting the bed, and he felt strengthened now by having his hero so close by!

And there could be no more beautiful example of the sensitivity to the human need for a hero to provide strength in times of vulnerability than the Make-A-Wish Foundation's generosity in giving seriously ill children the opportunity to spend time with a hero of their choice. And Dave has been chosen as this hero many times. Dave's physical presence has lifted the spirits and even softened the physical symptoms of sick children.

But as with the nutritional needs we have discussed, this food is not just for children. Adults, too, need the idealization nutrient. It's important for us to try to surround ourselves with people and ideas that we respect. Optimally we can build a broadening base of people we regard and look up to. I tell high school and college students to try to take the time to find mentors, teachers, special relatives, or even surrogate parent figures. I tell them to actively seek out people they respect who give them the feeling of self-respect. I can't think of a better investment of time for one's psyche. I assure people that they will feel better about *themselves* if they connect with people who have qualities that they would like to emulate. These can be personal qualities or they can be attributes such as having certain talents or knowing something special or interesting. It is very important to look for people whom you respect, who are happy in what they are doing, and who seem to have a high Vitality Pulse. Connect with those people. Learn from them. Treasure your time with them. We are helping you build your fiber.

As human beings, we are all prone to encountering disappointments in our heroes or people we have idealized. We can even become disillusioned with theories, philosophies or beliefs that we have held up as important or special. When these people or dearly held beliefs fail, we can actually become symptomatic. For example, many supporters of President Clinton became depressed when he was impeached, because they could no longer hold him in the same regard.

It is important to recognize that these symptoms were not just reactions about President Clinton. The individuals in Clinton's circle felt diminished themselves because of the disruption of their own need to be affiliated with someone for whom they could maintain admiration and idealization. This drop in self-esteem (or shame) can often be further compounded by the fact that when a person has idealized someone who has become famous, who then happens to fall in the public eye, opponents of the famous figure may delight in ridiculing the person who has idealized that figure. I witnessed this happen recently when my liberal friends ridiculed my conservative friends shortly after conservative radio personality Rush Limbaugh had his troubles with drug addiction so widely publicized. Look what happened to the Enron wives when their previously idealized executive husbands fell. Their own self-esteem fell. Were they not trying to heal their own injured self-esteem by seeking mirroring in appearing in *Playboy*?

There are many less dramatic examples in everyday life where a person's own self-esteem falls when someone he looks up to does something disappointing. An entire city can seem to become depressed if its team loses the Super Bowl or the World Series. Or when parents divorce, children often experience anxiety, depression and insecurity if their image of one or both of their parents has become tarnished in the process.

In addition, we can become symptomatic when we fall short of our *own* ideals. We are all vulnerable to setbacks in as many areas as one can imagine: dreams, aspirations, goals, or emotional investments. These can be investments in what one wants to become in the *outside* world, such as career, work, or intellectual achievement. Or they can be investments in how we want to be in our *internal* world, such as, "I always wanted to be an honest person"; "I always wanted to be a kind and empathetic person"; "I always wanted to be a person who is loyal, trustworthy and forgiving." The list can go on and on. These ideals are developed during childhood and held dearly into adulthood, often without any conscious awareness that we hold them. As core beliefs, these ideals are so ingrained within ourselves that we do not question them any more than we question the color of our eyes. They just *are* who we are, or who we hope to see ourselves as, as individuals.

An example I have seen often in my practice is couples who are going through the treatment of infertility. Often they have grown up picturing themselves with children and a family. When this does not happen, their ideal image becomes shattered and they are frequently in danger of feeling helplessness, depression and rage. Often these feelings, along with the disillusionment of a long-held ideal, cause the erosion of their own personal relationship. Many couples spend tens of thousands of dollars trying to grasp back their ideal of having a family. This need is so intense that they are willing to go through surgeries, take medications, or relentlessly pursue whatever new clinical option is available; picturing themselves without children is a shattered ideal – a culture shock.

Many people enter analysis suffering a crisis of *internal* ideals, though they may not articulate it as such. They may be wondering how long they should stay in an unhappy marriage or job. Often they are in pain because of the contrast between how they pictured their lives and what it actually feels like to be actually living it. Helping these individuals involves enabling them to consciously examine their background and the ideals they developed during childhood to help them, now, make judgments about the goals of their True Selves. They need to learn to differentiate between what their True Self needs and what others' expectations have been. They need to weigh their values, to assess what to do when their own internal ideals conflict with each other (such as having a bigger income versus having more time to be with one's family – the conflict with which Dave's grandfather dealt). Because long-held ideals are so strongly embedded, one can often not do this alone. Sorting through these conflicts of ideals is an arduous process, which requires heart-to-heart talks with a close friend or with the added expertise of a skilled therapist.

One woman came to me for treatment because she was in deep conflict about whether to leave her husband, whom she loved dearly. Because of his childhood issues, he was unable to enjoy any of her successes and became hostile and devaluing of her anytime she enjoyed a personal achievement, either socially or academically. Despite years of couples therapy, every time something good happened to her, he would become sadistic and cruel.

My patient was torn between her internal ideal of staying with a man she loved, and the competing ideal of wanting to progress in her life and to thrive. Also, as a devout Catholic, it was difficult for her even to consider divorce. After much hard work, she began to see that her True Self ultimately needed above all to be able to blossom and develop. She chose to honor this ideal and therefore made the painful decision to remove herself from the toxins of her interpersonal marital environment. This was her decision. Someone else might have sided with a different ideal according to the values of her own sense of self.

Dave faced a similar conflict. It was not until he had developed a serious illness that almost cost him his life that he realized he had to break out of a marriage that was not working. There had never been a divorce in Dave's family, and he had to balance his ideal of what was emotionally, mentally, and physically healthy for him with his ideal of regard for family tradition. Recognizing the message in his illness prompted him to realize the prevailing value he had about preserving his own life and vitality, even if that meant not doing what he thought was expected of him.

Making peace with the needs of one's True Self is important both psychologically and physically. There is an increasing amount of scientific evidence that emotional stressors can promote physical illness and the breakdown of the immune system. *Time* magazine (January 2003) printed articles entitled "The Power of Mood: Lifting Your Spirits Can Be Potent Medicine" and "Your Mind, Your Body: Doctors and Scientists Are Learning How Emotions Are Connected to Our Physical Health." And a February 2003 *Newsweek* cover story was on "Anxiety and Your Brain: How Living with Fear Affects Mind and Body."

In summary, one of the challenges of a successful life is learning how to discern when to keep pursuing the ideals one has long held (by taking advantage of known options in the external world and pressing one's self to the limit) and when to step back, reassess and redefine other ideals. Sometimes redefining our ideals and moving in a different direction can save our lives. The infertile couple might, perhaps, be able to reorient themselves around ways in which a child-free life might provide things that they would value or even learn to embrace and treasure. People who have had careers based on their physical prowess and then suffer an injury might redefine their ideal in terms of providing something valuable to themselves or to society in order to leave the dormant state and bloom again.

None of these are easy decisions to make. All change is loss and all loss requires a period of grieving and re-equilibrium. But mobilizing oneself to be active in striving for some ideal is truly the mark of a hero. After a setback, being able to hold onto the feeling that one can *do something*, regain some power or have some mastery over one's own fate is a critical life tool.

As you will recall, what first attracted me to Dave's movies was the way the Dave character could remobilize himself, recapture his self-esteem and continue on with the adventures of the stories without getting bogged down in feelings of inadequacy, guilt, shame or failure. When we examine the life stories of real heroes, we see people who have the ability to pick up their life tools and take action against the feeling of helplessness. To extend our budding flower metaphor, after "I shouldn't have done that," "you shouldn't have done that," or "life shouldn't have done that," they can collect their rake, their shovel, their trowel, and *work their garden*!

One inspiring example of this healthy kind of action can be seen in survivors of hostage situations or political prisons. (Dodes, p. 21) When these imprisoned people found secret ways to express an aspect of their identity, they found that they were able to preserve a sense of themselves. Sometimes they accomplished this by recalling events from their past, keeping track in their own way of their own history of imprisonment. But those who gave up all sense of personal power tended to sink into depression or die prematurely. The experience of these people underlies the fact that *acting* in some form when one is trapped and helpless is not only *normal*, it is psychologically *essential*.

So Dave's message is: If you are running over your dad's car when you're learning to drive a monster truck; if you're stranded in a rainstorm because you've forgotten to fill the gas tank on your motorcycle; if you've gotten lost on the highway because you've been reading your map upside down; or even if you've blown up a building by mistake because you pushed the wrong lever while learning to drive a bulldozer, you have a *choice*. You can sink into a feeling of helplessness, despair, or passive acceptance of defeat, or you can take some time to assess your feeling and responsibility, reorganize, pull yourself up by your bootstraps (or branches, roots and tendrils) so to speak, and activate a variety of future options.

Sometimes your best option may be just re-invoking your dream and trying to find alternative ways to make that dream, or those ideals, come true. But sometimes the option may be to re-evaluate your ideals, change direction and search for greener pastures. Whatever your path, resilience involves a focusing on tools, mastery and an active effort to regain a sense of vitality. The moral of the story is that no garden meant to thrive goes untended.

Now would be a good time to pick up your Psychological Nutrition Pyramid worksheet again and fill in some of your heroes and ideals. You might want to use different colored pencils for past ideals/heroes, present ideals/heroes, and maybe even future ideals/heroes. Find all the ones ripe for harvest.

## TWINSHIP

Another step up on the Psychological Nutrition Pyramid is the need for twinship – the need to have someone who resembles us or who is like us in one or more important ways. This is a need that starts in school-age children. Boys like boys and want to be like boys. Girls like girls and want to be like girls. Often the twain shall never meet. Hence the fear of getting the infamous "girl cooties."

This need for likeness can be seen most dramatically in adolescence because there are so many hormonal changes and general instabilities during this period of transition. Having someone who can be perceived as a twin provides a sense of strength or "we-ness" that shores up some of this sense of alienation and vulnerability. During the maelstrom of normal adolescence, the protection of twinship is made visibly evident in the propensity to wear the same fashions, pierce the same parts of the body, get similar tattoos, wear the same style of makeup, listen to the same music, and emulate the same movie stars and sports heroes – or perhaps to join the same "gang." In the anxious transition from childhood to adulthood, the need for somebody "like me" is in the foreground.

In some situations, however, the craving for twinship may be abnormally great, and lead to extreme and unusually radical actions. Oprah Winfrey featured discussions of these behaviors on her television show in early October 2003, where some of the drastic means some teenagers go to in order to fit into a group were discussed. Some of these behaviors are obviously abnormal: binge drinking, drugs, sex parties ("rainbow parties") and stealing to get the "in" clothing. One teen described body cutting. It is obvious in these extreme examples that the need for twinship is overemphasized because of other psychological factors. We can see cult behavior in the same light – an over-craving for a twinship nutrient that indicates deprivation in other nutritional areas on the Psychological Nutrition Pyramid and which clearly cries out for professional intervention.

As with the other needs, in adulthood, we still have twinship needs. We might belong to a political party in which people's ideas resemble ours, or we might belong to a professional society of like-minded people. We might root for the same team. Have you ever noticed what a fortifying and strengthening feeling it is to unexpectedly come upon someone who attended your college or who came from your hometown? And it has become a regular routine on talk shows for the crowd to shriek and whistle and clap when a particular city or state is mentioned.

When I was about 9 years old, I was small and blonde (I still am!), and my best friend (a year older) was tall and thin and brunette. We used to spend long hours sitting on a swing, on each other's laps, sitting face to face, one pair of legs going forward and the other pair of legs going back, swinging back and forth chanting in singsong voices, "Which is the front and which is the back; which is the front and which is the back?" As I look back on this, I see our act as a perfect metaphor of the two of us (one short and blonde, one tall and dark), linked in imagination as twins.

Today, I still enjoy this twinship feeling with my niece, Lauren, who is *40 years* younger than I. She also is tall and dark, yet we still share all kinds of "twinship" experiences that we build together. We have matching rings that "twin us" with my mother (her grandmother). We buy odd matching things to wear (such as garish gold shoes that we would never think of wearing other than to a family function). And we indulge in these *for no other reason* than to feel like twins. If you are female, you probably remember a fond feeling about friendship rings or school rings. If you are male, you may feel the same thing about a fraternity pin, paddle, or secret handshake.

Our need for twinship never ends. There is now a group for middle-aged women called the Purple Hat Society, based on the poem *Warning, When I Am an Old Woman I Shall Wear Purple* by Jenny Joseph. The mission of this group is to encourage middle-aged women to feel connected, and to join in abandoning some of their previous emotional restrictions. The banner color of purple concretizes their bond of sameness of purpose as well as their stronger need for twinship during the transition period of middle age.

For people who have spent an extended period of time in a foreign country, unable to find anyone who physically resembles them or speaks their language, a feeling of alienation begins to emerge. This is a twinship deprivation. No one looks or sounds like you! When you find someone who is your nationality, speaks your language, or has hair or skin color the same as your own, there is a nameless sense of relief and security. But since twinship is an inner experience of feeling as if someone resembles you, it can be something known only to the *twins* themselves. It does not need to be externally identifiable to an outside observer (remember my dark-haired friend and me on the swings). It is the *feeling* that someone shares a likeness with us. And when this twinship need is met, there is a powerful rush of confidence that enhances a person's sense of well-being and self-worth.

An example is a woman I know, Kersti, in her late 50s who was born in Estonia and whose family immigrated to the United States because of the Russian Communists. She described growing up in U.S. culture, always having a subtle lonely feeling: "not isolated," she said, but "knowing that you're different in many ways, but not totally different. There was always a quality of missing something, or part of me missing." She noted that with many immigrants they had to leave their trade skills and qualifications behind. Some were retrained in the States and found a niche, but others did not. Her parents did not, so she felt that she never fit in.

When she was 27 she decided to give her mother a treat and take her back to Estonia to see her extended family, many of whom had recently returned from the gulag prison camps in Siberia. Although they had written to each other, this was the first time her mother had personally seen her family. While Kersti thought that she was doing her mother the favor, she did not realize how elevating it would be for *her* to be introduced to people of her own nationality. "Hearing the mother tongue" overwhelmed her with an unexpected feeling of belonging. Seeing their Nordic faces and realizing that similarities exist and that there were "shared qualities" gave her a welcomed emotional boost. She described it as "an embracing feeling" and "an unexpectedly heartwarming feeling of mutual interest and curiosity." She described how sad it was to "have to leave these people behind, sad to say goodbye," with "no idea if I would ever have *that feeling* again."

We never know when a person might provide a twinship experience, and sometimes we are delightfully surprised. A pastor I know does consultations in his kitchen. He wants to eliminate the power imbalance so that his parishioners will feel comfortable talking to him. He sets up placemats and chairs at the kitchen table and serves coffee. One of his new parishioners came in to talk to him and said, "Oh, you have the same pattern on your placemat as I do in my kitchen!" She suddenly relaxed, sat down, and began to openly tell him her troubles.

For anyone who has participated in Alcoholics Anonymous (AA), or other 12-step support groups, the healing power of twinship experiences is almost palpable. Whether it is being with advanced breast cancer survivors, as documented by Dr. David Spiegel at Stanford University, or people who share problems of overeating, sexual addictions, compulsive gambling, compulsive spending, and now even such things as compulsive Internet use, the power twinship experiences can provide is undeniable. I felt this in a small way myself only the other day when I had to have a minor medical procedure – four, rather short, intravenous infusions in a medical center to break a nasty grip of resistant cluster migraine headaches that would just not go away. I spent two hours a day in a clean and well-lit room with six other people, all being treated for far more serious conditions than my own, such as a brain tumor, myasthenia gravis and stroke. Although we were there for very different reasons, we developed an affectionate bond, even a support system, as we sat there together, all in the same chairs, all sipping our coffee, all watching *Ellen* on TV, and all bound to our chairs, sharing our vulnerability, plugged into our IV's. Differences in genders, differences in ages, differences in medical diagnoses, all faded away as we "twinned" together for these four days brought together in the sameness of our situation and feeling an increasing attachment to each other.

The Dave movies are brimming with twinship examples, especially the ones where Dave and Becky play off each other as if they were kids of the same age. And for children, watching Dave is like watching a twin of themselves. Although Dave is doing very grown-up things, he portrays himself as if he were struggling with the same issues and feelings as a 5-year-old – the desire to learn, the unabashed awe at heroes and big vehicles, flashes of shyness and insecurity at approaching that "bigness," and a strong drive to be able to master grown-up situations and to feel competent. In fact, "kids" of *any age* can identify with Dave's anxieties about new challenges, his shyness in the face of new adventures, and his underlying desire to excel and to learn. Even adults to whom I have shown the movies have remarked, "I *like* this guy Dave; he has problems just like mine!" And part of Dave's success in his movies is that he presents himself as someone most viewers can "twin with" very easily. We *all* know what it feels like to take on a task, or machine, that first appears daunting, to take a leap toward our dream, then maybe to flub up, to falter, to fall, to fail (or even to bear the fear of failing), and then to rise up to the challenge of continuing on.

A friend of mine, noting the twinship in the Dave and Becky adventures, talked nostalgically to me about her own experience growing up in a neighborhood where there were often real home construction sites next door or around the block. She remembered, back in the 1960s, that at the end of the workday, the kids looked forward to the adventure of exploring the dump trucks and bulldozers that were left for the night. No one made them stay away! (Those days must have been before construction sites were partitioned off due to fear of injury and liability issues). My friend's face glowed with nostalgia as she recalled the adventures she had with her friends and the sense of excitement, independence and exploration they shared together. She beamed as she told me how very big and grown-up she and her friends felt climbing on the huge machines *together* – feeling safe all the time since they knew that their homes were nearby.

It is interesting that Dave and I share a twinship about our favorite children's books: *The Little Engine That Could* (Watty Piper, 1961); *Scuffy the Tug Boat* (Gertrude Crampton, 1955); *Katy and the Big Snow* (Virginia Lee Burton, 1943); *Oh, The Places You'll Go* (Dr. Seuss, 1990); *I Knew You Could* (Platt & Munk, 2003); and *Mike Mulligan and His Steam Shovel* (Virginia Lee Burton, 1977), all of which focus on the theme of facing adversity and pushing through it. In a way we have been twins since our own childhoods – long before we ever knew each other – at least in terms of being drawn to stories about recovery from adversity or "bouncing back."

In terms of childhood twinning, one of my favorite Dave stories is *There Goes a Rollercoaster* where Dave's "son" is determined to help his serious-minded father "find the kid" in him again. In this video, we watch a carefully programmed "lesson plan" in which the son lures his father away from very adult work at his computer to explore all the excitements of a huge amusement park. There, the father is systematically retrained by his son to be able to renounce his adult concerns and worries so he can free himself from the shackles of adult responsibility and indulge in the thrills and delights of childhood once again with his son – now his alter ego.

After multiple trials, his son exclaims proudly, "Now he's got it!" as he witnesses his father goofing around, balancing himself on the edge of a curb and nonchalantly chomping on a pastry stick.

Twining with the enthusiasm and unencumbered joy of childhood is much of the allure of all of Dave's movies. He captures the audience with humor. He engages us in recapturing the wonders of childhood before inhibition, self-consciousness, self-criticism and self-editing take over. Dave's movies remind us that child*ish* and child*like* are not the same. We *all* long to recapture the twinship feeling; and, along with it, the exuberance and vitality of childhood. The "Dave" character, by the very essence of his child*like* nature, provides us with this makeup.

Now take out your pyramid worksheet and fill in the names of people with whom you feel a special kinship or likeness. These could be people who have some quality that resembles yours. They don't have to be people who are completely like you, but they should *share something* with you that is special enough that when you're together you get a feeling of vitality. This can be someone you know, someone you have known in the past with whom you would like to reconnect, or someone you do not know very well now but whom you would like to know better.

## SPARRING

At the very top of the Psychological Nutrition Pyramid is the need to spar. This is the need we all have to bump up against someone, to differ, to wrestle, to challenge and be challenged. We see this most concretely in young children as they roughhouse with each other on the playground, or with the family dog on the kitchen floor or with their parents on the living room floor or with each other in pillow fights. We see it in teenagers at the dining room table when they debate issues with their parents and with other family members in an attempt to delineate their positions and define who they are, differentiating themselves from others. Teens often need to clash with and oppose others to form and develop their own ideas. We see the need for sparring in adulthood when people forcefully, sometimes almost antagonistically, come at each other in discussions of politics, religion, or other dearly held beliefs.

In fact, by the time you get to sparring you have to have had all the other nutrients in the bottom part of the triangle or sparring could turn into destructiveness. If you *have* had all the other nutrients, you will be strong enough to allow another person to be different and you will enjoy a healthy, back-and-forth interchange. You will be strong enough to enjoy differences. In these interchanges, if all goes well, both participants end up feeling invigorated.

Again, our society intuitively knows about sparring. Witness expressions such as: "we've met our match," or "he'll give you a run for your money." A friend of mine calls her husband "my worthy opponent." The British Parliament has "the loyal opposition." (At times, I call my own husband this!)

It is the sparring type of interchange that helps competitors hone their skills. It helps individuals create and shape a self-definition and identity. As long as no one is injured or overcome by the adversary, each is stimulated to grow from the opportunity to spar, much as two well-matched tennis players can refine their games by playing with each other (rather than by playing with someone markedly superior or inferior). We all need a bit of this healthy "to-and-fro" in our diet. Often there is too much sparring in the diet and too little of the other food groups, in the same way that there is too much fat and sugar and too little of the other nutrients in one's biological diet. In fact, it is almost a given that if there has been deprivation of connectedness, mirroring, affirmation, idealization, heroes or twinship, there will most assuredly be an overabundance of sparring. The reason for this is that sparring (sometimes called aversiveness) is often used as a defense mechanism to make people feel stronger when their sense of self-esteem is weak. When people are hungry, they are in a weakened state. Acting pugnacious is a cover. It makes the person, and others, more likely to perceive them as strong.

Continuing with the metaphor of the flower, it makes sense then that if the basic nutrients of connectedness, idealization and twinship have not been provided, the organism will, by definition, be weak and hungry. With humans, this means that a person will be vulnerable to feeling shame and a sense of defectiveness. His view of himself will be that there is something wrong with him. So he will resort to sparring in an attempt to cover up such feelings. This is because, in many ways, it is more comfortable to feel angry, strong and powerful, than to feel weak and vulnerable. Unfortunately, sparring can escalate out of control to rage and aggression. When someone comes to me with an inordinate amount of anger, it is always a tip-off to me as a clinician that there is a great deal of emotional hurt, insecurity, and feeling of weakness underneath. An overload of sparring in one's diet is always an indication that there has been a deprivation in the other four basic Psychological Food Groups.

I once had a patient in therapy who pushed me and taunted me. It was as if he was always trying to start a fight. The sparring ceased to be stimulating. I felt overpowered. He had a strong need to provoke me, to spar with me, to differ with me, to be sarcastic with me, and even to try to get a rise out of me by calling me names. Upon examination of his history, we discovered that he had had a very sadistic, alcoholic father who was both emotionally and physically abusive. In addition, he had had fairly severe emotional and financial deprivation. All of these factors contributed to his feeling of not being special and his conviction that he could hold no hope for ever becoming anyone of substance or importance.

During our work together, my patient slowly began to build a different self-image and to start to recognize some aspects of his personality as worthwhile and even valuable. He met a woman, was able to court her, married her and had a child. His irritability settled down and he was promoted to a manager within the company in which he worked. He still remained vulnerable to having drops in his self-esteem when he became frustrated or felt slighted, but his confidence grew stronger and stronger. In the treatment with me, he became able to listen to my comments without the need to spar taking center stage. He began to ask for my opinion on things and no longer had the automatic reaction of having to negate, push up against, or block my input.

From this above description, I imagine that I need not say that it was very difficult for me to sit with this man for the early part of the treatment. Typically, most people can absorb only so much sparring, just as they can metabolize only so much fat in their diet. Only so much can be stomached before you, yourself, start to feel sick. But a certain amount of sparring can be like a good spice – very vitalizing. We see this in competitive classroom situations, sports, and political campaigns. As long as sparring can be done with wholesome vigor, with no one person collapsing, and no one person becoming the victimizer, sparring can lead to all sorts of enlivening outcomes.

In Dave's movies, Dave and Becky provide many models of healthy sparring. One of my personal favorites is in *There Goes a Monster Truck* when they have to endure so many frustrations in their effort to get the truck to the convention center for the monster truck competition. They have words; they bicker; they even scold each other a bit. Ultimately, after failing to deliver the truck to the competition, they end up in an actual wrestling match in a mud pit. But, each person in this dynamic duo ends up only feeling closer and more involved. The message remains crystal clear, however. As Becky and Dave stand breathless and covered with mud, neither would desire a steady diet of this kind of relating.

Yet, they play together with sparring on a regular basis. In *There Goes a Garbage Truck* Becky, squealing all the way, gets scooped up by Dave who is so excited about learning to drive the truck that he is oblivious to where she is until she emerges from the garbage pile, shrieking with some unidentifiable junk stuck in her hair. In another episode Becky plays a trick on Dave when she uses a crane to unexpectedly lift him high into the air on a hook when he's trying to learn about rescue equipment. And in Dave's other episodes Dave and Becky wrestle with snakes, throw mud at each other, toss tires back and forth at each other, all reveling in stimulating horseplay. The central point is that no one ever gets hurt or seriously humiliated or overpowered, and the sparring is always only a small part of the Dave and Becky adventures.

The point to learn here is that it is important that parents let their children play with and explore their need to spar by being willing to wrestle with them through ideas – or even physically – without there being an "overwhelmer" or an "overwhelmee"; "a collapsed" and "victor." Children need to "develop their muscles," so to speak, without threat of injury to either party. This is because it takes musculature and endurance for success, confidence, growth and vitality. Children have to *learn* to fight fairly without one having to succumb to, or be squashed by, the force of ideas or personality of another person. Healthy sparring communicates that one does not have to collapse for the other to feel victorious. Both can end up feeling vital and energized. Also to feel victorious, your partner does not have to be brought down. To extend our metaphor, healthy tree branches must be able to flex in a strong wind – not to break.

In high school, Dave had a teacher of philosophy, Mr. Kenny, who encouraged him to study debate. This gifted teacher challenged Dave to develop his ideas and his own self-definition through this form of disciplined and structured sparring. In another example of sparring, my father and brother used to energetically chase each other around the house, playfully striking out with what they called "glancing blows" with their feet, to see who could strike first – shrieking with laughter and feeling deeply engaged with each other and excited. During these games the intensity of interchange was so great that it was like no one else was in the house but the two of them. Both took "winning" and "losing" in stride. Both felt empowered and because the ritual was done with mutual love, respect, and limits, it never alienated one from the other but only augmented their feeling of closeness and involvement – as the memories of today still do.

Another example of healthy sparring was told to me by a nun who was giving Bible school lessons to teenagers. After they had worked very hard at helping the younger students pay attention, learn and put away their materials, they asked the 60-year-old nun to come over to their car. With a twinkle in their eye, they showed her a big bucket full of water balloons they had sequestered in the front seat. The teenagers knew that their intention to throw these water balloons on the church lawn was a bit off limits, but the wise and loving nun in a frustrating situation could empathize with their need to spar after working so hard with the younger students. Her eyes twinkled back at them. She told them that they could go behind the rectory after everyone had left the property because she knew that they needed to let off some steam. After all, they had been very accommodating and patient with the younger children. The appreciation the nun showed for these teenagers' need for sparring cemented their admiration of and attachment to her and is probably a big reason they continue to come to church activities.

Another example of sparring comes from my family and also became a ritual. When my brother was about 10 years old he hated having his hair cut. He had fine blonde hair, just like mine, and always liked to have it cut in a brush cut. Each time his hair was cut, however, he thought it was cut much *too short*, and when my father drove him home from the barber they went through the same old routine: my father would ask, "Rick, how do you like your haircut?" My brother would reply "I don't like it!" My father would lovingly reach out his hand to pat his knee and my brother would extend his own hand over my father's and they would do a mock boxing match with their hands, one against the other, all the way home. This sparring ritual was always in jest, and always with warmth and these nasty, awful haircuts were looked forward to every month.

A very concrete example of sparring is that of a little girl I know who was born with only one arm. As a baby, she got her first prosthesis; it looked like a plastic arm. But her second prosthesis had a metal pincher at the end. She liked to entertain her cousins by crushing cans. She wrote, "My arm is a powerhouse. When I was younger, all I had to do was claw with one arm, grab treats from a piñata, carry all the Christmas presents to my room and fight with my brother with it. I was always looking for a new challenge, so I decided to learn karate. I was excellent at it and loved sparring. I was quick, strong, and fearless. I even broke thick, wooden boards with my hand. I learned that fake arms can be scary but fun.'" (Story courtesy of my friend Noelle Trometer, age 13) What a wonderful example this is of self-definition, self-delineation and the healthy need for a feeling of enhancement, of potency in a girl who could have felt handicapped – all through the healthily managed use of sparring.

Sparring is a form of vigorous *interactivity*. It can be done physically, verbally, or even non-verbally. One can feel the "to and fro" in some people, such as Dave. The vitality in Dave's whole bodily presence enhances his sense of engagement with people with whom he is communicating – especially children. It seems to me that that rhythmic interactiveness, in which he seems to lean forth and touch the world, touches the hearts of children. It conveys an emotional accessibility that is a model for what we all need – especially children. I have witnessed the part of Dave's personality that involves the needs to joke, to touch, to be playful, to "hit the ball back," and to physically engage. And his family told me that since his preteen years, he has always loved rough-and-tumble activities. He literally enjoyed bumping up against his environment on his bicycle to the point that he was characterized as a "hell raiser." Perhaps a better name for him would have been a "raiser of people's spirits."

When I first met Dave in person, it was easy to sense his physical vibrancy. Within 30 seconds of greeting me, he threw his arms around me and gave me a big bear hug, evaporating any anxiety I might have had about meeting him. Not only on screen, but also in real life, I imagine that Dave could be the "poster child" for an ad for AT&T that says "Reach out and touch someone."

So, although it is at the top of the pyramid, the need for sparring is an essential nutrient for psychological health and well-being. Take out your pyramid worksheet and enter the names of people or activities that give you some feeling of "push/pull." These can be physical or mental, or even nonverbal, such as something to do with body language. You will know you are getting the sparring nutritional ingredient if you get an invigorating sense of being interacted with and bumped up against. Perhaps we can say that flirting back and forth can be seen as a form of sparring, too!

To close this chapter I would like to quote a conversation I had with a very insightful patient of mine who described:

"The 'deprived child' can be a 'child' in any point of life because deprivation is the lack of the nourishment we need and we never move into a time or space in life where we don't need these things. I came from a loving home and I entered a deprived environment. How does one accommodate oneself to a deprived life? There are only two ways," he said to me, "one is you can accommodate, do things to be included that are not your True Self and live a false and flawed existence.

"The second is you can move into extreme hostility. Some people become suicidal or homicidal at the slightest provocation. Homicidal because the slightest thing can give them a flashback of their own deprivation if they ever had it earlier on. So they overreact, or they can act out sexually, violently, or abusively because they can't deal with the flashbacks of being deprived. They can fight or they can go into flight, go into resistance, hostility, anger, and withdrawal. I guess my pattern of accommodation is better."

I said to this gentleman, no, you are missing a third thing. You can acknowledge that you *do* have needs. Maybe you won't find them in this particular environment. Maybe you have to physically remain in this environment for the reasons that you choose, but maybe you can find these needs and have them met in different environments – in music, in sports, in creativity, with friends, with other colleagues you know or have not yet met. You can think about whether you want to change your primary environment, but if you really feel there are reasons not to do so, I'm sure you can find the creativity to meet your needs. All you must do is come to the point where you realize, within your soul, that your needs are *valid*.

# CHAPTER 6

## PURPOSE AND INTEGRITY

I was discussing our Psychological Nutritional Pyramid with a wealthy, good-looking, physically fit, intelligent and psychologically minded patient of mine. He said,

"Doc, I *have* all these five Psychological Food Groups, and yet, I'm still not happy. You need to add something else. You need to put a circle around the whole triangle, a circle about having a purpose for your life, or having some philosophy that directs your life. While I have every nutrient in this food triangle, I'm not totally happy because I retired so early and now, as yet, I no longer can see any purpose for myself."

Now, at the risk of sounding like one of Dave's *There Goes a...* stories, I think that I could say that *I*, Dr. Carol, have the best job in the world. Every day my clinical work enriches and expands my knowledge of the human condition. I cannot deny that this particular patient of mine who made these above comments has enlightened me about this issue (as well as many other issues) and has, by so doing, enriched not only this book but me too.

The sense of having a purpose or a guiding philosophy is extremely important to a person's self-image and sense of vitality. Finding a purpose or a value system gives direction to one's life and helps us choose from the menu of options available to us. The ability to choose options that are consonant with our values serves to structure our being and defines our sense of who we are. It is what makes up our integrity.

Dave has said that "nothing figures more prominently in causing depression than being without goals; nothing is more stressful than having a goal, but not taking the steps to accomplish it." Having a purpose in life has a profound effect on who we feel we are.

Dr. Steven Reiss, in his book *Who Am I?* (2002), contrasted "feel-good happiness" with "value-based happiness." He said that pleasant sensations and sensual feelings cause "feel-good happiness," but these feelings are short-lived because they do not provide inner meaning. By contrast, "value-based happiness" comes from life, it is long-lasting and more within the individual's control. Bonnano (2004) asserts that:

> "Armed with this set of beliefs, hardy individuals have been found to appraise potentially stressful situations as less threatening, thus minimizing the experience of distress. Hardy individuals are also more confident and better able to use active coping and social support, thus helping them deal with the distress they do experience." (Florian, Mikulincer & Taubman, 1995)

If people believe that they can grow and find purpose in their lives, having or re-tending a goal that is valued provides a meaning and purpose to one's life. In the January/February 2001 issue of

*Psychology Today* Reiss said, "You can find value-based happiness if you are rich or poor, smart or mentally challenged, athletic, popular or socially awkward... Everybody has the potential to live in accordance with their values... Wealthy people are not necessarily happy, and poor people are not necessarily unhappy."

Dave and I would add that having a purpose provides a needed compass for the myriad of choices and opportunities that life offers at its various crossroads. Dave would add, in his noteworthy optimistic nature, that most people in life fail not because they couldn't come up with a purpose, a motivation, or a "guiding light," but because they have lacked the positive energy or motivation to follow through.

And as with your car battery that has gone dead, motivation must often be jump-started with the help of someone else. Unfortunately, these needed jumper cables are often not available. Society seems to be so busy entertaining children that we have neglected to inspire them to have a purpose or help ignite their dreams. Many children are so driftless that they can't even answer the question, "What did you do this summer?" How sad, since the feeling of competency, or having the feeling that we can *do* something and have a purpose, is a central component to a child's self-image.

In terms of purpose, child therapist Cynthia Feigel maintains that it is crucial for children to feel that they are *useful* to other people and especially that adults need their strengths and talents. She suggests, for example, that if our children are musical, we might encourage them to choose music for a dinner party; if teenagers tend to pick creative color combinations for their clothing, we might let them offer consultation on colors for a bathroom or other parts of the home. The central point is that children need to get the feeling that their strengths are an *asset* to the adult world. This confidence will make it more likely that they will come to envision themselves as someone who has the ability to grow up and contribute to society – to become a real taxpayer!

If people have a purpose, by definition, they have a sense of worth. Having a sense of purpose gives an internal focus so that you can set your own direction according to your own core values and not be susceptible to the influence of any stray person who may cross your path. This is truly the definition of integrity – the ability to hold on to your *own* direction, your *own* compass, your *own* value system, your *own* sense of self, your True Self, in the face of pushes and pulls from outside oneself. As the little pig said to the wolf outside, "You can huff and puff but you can't blow *my* house down."

In fact, much of life's satisfaction comes from being absorbed in purposeful activity when we forget about our own problems and lose track of time. Mihaly Csikszentmihalyi calls this phenomenon "flow." This state can occur in any activity, but to qualify as "flow," it needs to be something one loves to do, especially if the activity feels like a combination of work and play. According to positivity psychologist Martin Seligman, everyone has what he calls "a signature strength." People *feel* best when they are doing what they *do* best. Seligman says we are happiest when we are "playing to our strengths."

In his movies, Dave seems to be enthusiastically doing what he *loves*. And watching the movies children (and adults) in the audience imaginatively "play along with him" in these grown-up tasks. We learn to drive big trucks, fly airplanes and spaceships, and navigate a train along the tracks. When Dave learns to drive a bulldozer, fly a spaceship, manage a monster truck, race a motorcycle, handle a race car, etc. he is offering children hope – a model with which to identify. This model is often portrayed in a dream state, after Dave has gotten knocked on the head in one of his misadventures. But Dave's message is always about showing children that they can "think big"; they can "do it" in their imaginary future self.

Parents need to make efforts to convey the message, "I trust you with grown-up things." It is a message that gets internalized by the child as a prototype or template. Parents can build on this foundation to give their children the confidence that they can have goals and grow up to become whatever the child envisions as "big." This message stretches and motivates the youngsters' mind and spirit. Dave models "greatness" in the way Mark Twain suggested: "The really great make you feel that you, too, can become great."

As an example, in the story *The Horse Whisperer* a man creates a success where the opportunity did not exist before (or was only a nascent bud). He does this by inviting a girl who has a badly injured leg to drive a truck. Though she is stunned and convinced she can't do it, she ultimately surprises herself by driving. This man's trust in her ignited the pilot light of her confidence and lit up a feeling of empowerment she never expected. Renewed with a sense of competency and purpose, she was able to bounce back from the effects of the accident that had snuffed out the self she had known. She could even drive without monitoring. With the empathy and encouragement of this man, she could feel alive again. He was there for her at the right time and the right place, and with the right message.

Another example of someone being there at the right time to help instill purpose is a very intuitive patient of mine, who happened to be a schoolteacher. When she recognized that her own 5-year-old daughter was starting to become fearful of going to school, she fabricated a story to engage her daughter in "a mission." She told her daughter that because she, herself, worked in the school she knew that there was a little girl in her daughter's class who was frightened about being in school and would need her daughter's help and support. She said that that little girl had never been away from home before and that she was especially lonely and "could use a friend." Right before the mother's eyes, her daughter scooted out the door and onto the school bus, eagerly searching out whatever child she could find who looked like she might need a buddy. When mother and daughter met at home that evening, the daughter was aglow. She had, indeed, connected with some little classmate who had looked forlorn, and the two of them had spent the day together playing in the playground and jumping rope. All signs of school phobia had evaporated.

Sometimes, when my son, Grant, feels sad and anxious about my leaving to go to my office in the morning, I tell him that "I'm going to go help fix a 'boo,'" and I ask him for his advice on how I should do that. He does not yet understand the difference yet between his pediatrician doctor who helps fix actual "boo-boos," and a therapist doctor who helps patients with feelings that hurt; so, I blend the two types of hurts into the same sort of pain because, actually, emotional pain does feel like physical pain. For example, I pretend that I have a patient coming to see me who has a twisted arm or a broken leg. I mimic with my body how this might look. Grant loves to show me how to straighten out the arm or leg by altering its position and telling me that I should "hold it in place like that for 10 hours!" After we have worked out the technicalities of these treatment plans, Grants seems miraculously to lose all separation anxiety and happily lets me leave for work. He feels empowered by his ability to teach Mom how to help her patient. He feels strong and purposeful – no longer weak and vulnerable as the thought of separating from Mom had first left him.

Another value transmitted in Dave's movies has to do with his repetitive focus on "doing the right thing" and having positive ethics. He delightfully illustrates what is the central human conflict. How do we balance our conflicting loyalties between "doing what we *want* to do" and doing "what we *should* do" for ourselves and for others (having integrity)?

Both Dave's sister and mother told me that Dave took very seriously, early on, the responsibility of watching out for his baby sister. From the moment she came home from the hospital, he wanted to hold her and he felt it was his job to keep her safe. He did the right thing by her from day one. Dave's sister remembers the first time they went to the ocean together. She ran towards the water, and Dave came charging after her to rescue her. (Perhaps this is the origin of the *There Goes a Rescue Vehicle* scene in which Dave trundles into the water, tripping over his fins and his surfboard, getting tangled in seaweed and ending up totally embarrassed, all because he has been overly conscientious and has mistaken some unknown object bobbing in the water for a person in danger.)

But despite this high level of responsibility to others in his life and his movies, Dave's appeal is that he remains identifiably human. We can see him struggle with childlike impulses to do what *he* wants, rather impulsively, versus doing what he *should* be doing in an orderly fashion, as a grown-up. We are amused because we can identify with this struggle. In many episodes he struggles between his childlike impulses to ignore the teachers, to be impulsive, and not to listen to the instructor. In one of the episodes he does not listen to the train conductor, causing the train to go backwards. In another episode he doesn't listen to directions at the space center and gets knocked out during his unauthorized entry into the orbiter. Dave is constantly having to bounce back from all sorts of mishaps that befall him due to his giving in to these childlike impulses. We sympathize for him when he grandiosely ignores the instruction of the racecar driver in *There Goes a Racecar* causing him to spin off the road and crash into a haystack, enabling Becky to win the trophy. We cringe when he doesn't pay close enough attention to Frank, the monster truck instructor in *There Goes a Monster Truck*, causing him to drive over and crush his father's car.

At the same time, Dave's movies also show his clear "grown up" pro-social inclination. He was very upset and chagrined when he realized that because of carelessness he might not be able to get the monster truck to the competition on time, and he was even willing to work in the mud pit as his atonement for disappointing the people who were expecting him. In *There Goes a Spaceship* Dave instinctively knew that the right thing to do was to reserve the best part of the candy bar for his partner, Becky, when they ended up stranded in the wilderness after their spaceship careened out of control and crashed on what they thought was an alien planet. In *There Goes a Rescue Vehicle* it was natural for Dave to apologize to Becky after snapping at her in frustration when he felt frazzled and upset having been hoisted in a basket up a hill and bumped around on bushes and overgrowth.

Some people who have viewed only a part of one of Dave's movies have said, "How do you know that Dave's mantra, Shouldn't have done that, doesn't really advocate "you can do anything you want; you are free; consequences don't matter"? To this, I answer, "Wait! You have to watch the *whole movie!*" And I can make these comments with confidence as I've watched all the movies at least 15 times. In all of Dave's movies he demonstrates a *balance* between the needs of one's self and one's responsibility to others. His attitude is never flippant or sarcastic or dismissive. The pain on his face shows his repentance. He always accepts the consequences for his "shouldn't a done" and he never fails to articulate the moral learned by the story.

In fact, self-esteem has been defined by some scholars as the capacity "to appreciate our own worth and importance, to be accountable for ourselves *and* to act responsibly towards others." This quotation is from the 1990 California Taskforce to promote self-esteem and personal social responsibility.

Dave's stories colorfully and humorously illuminate this human struggle. We *all* negotiate between our childlike selves that, in grown-up ways, we have learned to control. We have learned to modulate our impulses and to delay gratification. The conflict between impulsivity, such as "tuning out" the instructor or clumsily not paying attention (so that food dumps on the table and on top of the head of a customer in *There Goes a Train*), provides a silly and humorous contrast to the prudence and carefulness that adults try to teach children on a daily basis (and to remember themselves).

For both children and adults, especially when we are tired, hungry, frustrated or worn down, acting grown-up and keeping on our "party manners" can be quite a strain. And in times of crisis or exhaustion even adults have to remind themselves to step back, listen to the instructor, ask for help, and start with small tasks.

Dave outlines these coping skills in all of his movies. He repetitively teaches themes such as "It's important to listen to the instructor," "It's good to ask for help," "Start with small garbage trucks before you learn about big garbage trucks." The truth is that restraint isn't easily learned for any of us. And when you go yourself to one of Dave's live shows, you'll see for yourself how tempting it is to want to take on the very biggest truck first!

But the main point here is that in all of Dave's movies pro-social values always win out, and the best part is that they are conveyed in easy-to-digest and very palatable ways. They are never served up in a pompous lecturing manner that "talks down" to children." In fact, in my first conversation with Dave by phone he told me that "not talking down to children" has always been his first priority. He hates it when "children are talked to like puppies." And, for me, as a psychoanalyst who has become very aware of the erosive effect of shame on the developing self, I would say that if you gain nothing else from this book than Dave's comment, "Don't talk down to children" you have harvested a prize-winning rose.

In summary, respect for others, integrity and kindness are values which are conveyed in the subcontext of Dave's adventure stories, but it is Dave's creative, playful and amusing means of transmission that makes them so easy to metabolize. Even in heated moments, when there is a conflict between "selfishness" versus "altruism," nothing demeaning or disparaging is ever conveyed and respect for the self *and* the other is always maintained – what a refreshing model for interpersonal and family interactions. This abiding attitude validates the belief of Rabbi Charles Shalman, "He who is the most gracious wins."

To quote from marriage and family therapist Dr. Laura Schlessinger,

A grandfather was talking to his grandson. "Grandson," he said, "there are two wolves living in my heart and they are at war with each other. One is vicious and cruel, the other is wise and kind."

"Grandfather," said the alarmed grandson, "which one will win?"

"The one I feed," said the grandfather.

A dear friend and esteemed scholar in the field of contemporary psychoanalysis, Dr. Malcolm Slavin, has written a great deal about the point that *all* human interactions involve working out conflicts of interest. When looked at from this viewpoint, much of the pain within families can be seen as due to ways of coping with these conflicts. All too frequently such natural tensions degenerate into rage, disrespect, shaming, and polarization into a "winner" and a "loser" – a "victim" and a "victimizer." The soothing message in Dave's movies is that *despite* normal tensions and interpersonal conflicts everyone maintains respect for themselves and the other. There is no ridicule and denigration as is seen in other cartoons that are supposed to be amusing.

Dave playfully models pro-social behavior sometimes by goofing up, and sometimes by "doing it right." But the main theme is that he never fails to take responsibility and ownership for the times he "shouldn't have done that." And his own personal life philosophy has the same theme: He advises, "I suggest you take on the responsibility of contributing while you are capable, and say to yourself, 'I am a *link* on a chain, I can either be a missing one, a weak one, or a strong one.'" I love this quote.

Dave had a situation in his own life where his sense of loyalty and responsibility made him return to a job at his radio station because he knew his employer was depending on him. This sense of loyalty actually cost him the opportunity to remain for further auditioning for the television show that he very much wanted to be on. But the value of "doing the right thing" and having good ethics was so ingrained in Dave's personality that he forfeited his own needs. Instead of doing what he wanted, he chose the path of integrity and responsibility to his employer.

Dave's sense of loyalty and responsibility literally could have killed him when he tenaciously continued filming a segment for *PM Magazine* during hazardous weather conditions in the Royal Gorge in Colorado in the midst of raging waterfalls. The film crew was set up for the shoot, but there were warnings from the local officials: rain had raised the water level to an all-time high. Dave decided to press on even though the rapids were 6+ rated. (There can be such a thing as too much devotion.)

Another one of the core values that runs throughout the Dave movies is the value of self-discipline and learning. When one reads about the journey of Dave's career, one is struck by his openness to learning, trying new things and self-expansion. His movies constantly emphasize learning safety, respect for equipment, and an idealization of mastery and competence. Dave is so enthusiastic about this principle that in his movie *Real Adventures: That's How They Do It... Chocolate*, he tells the bird "You should think every day!"

All of Dave's movies explicitly advocate studying hard and learning. At the end of *every* movie Dave encourages children to explore more about the career presented by "visiting their local library." Each movie ends with an expert lauding his career and telling children that they too can have the same career if they "stay in school and study." Here it is: an idealizable figure telling children that they, too, can reach the same goal. The gap is not unbridgeable. With serious intentions and effort, the child can be like the admired figure. And, the admired figure always *loves* the work that he does. This is a wonderful example of how idealization should work!

And Dave offers more for children about how to reach performance goals. He advocates respect for teachers and for authority figures. His movies extol the value of being patient, being willing to take small steps, and paying attention even when the small steps might be boring. Holding this philosophy within his own heart has certainly opened doors for Dave himself. As a schoolboy, while beginning to craft his entertaining abilities by dressing up and performing for his fellow students and teachers on holidays, Dave was also plugging away at his studies. After completing five years at Stevenson Elementary School, he was honored with the coveted "citizen award" – what wonderful recognition for his blossoming value of integrity.

Dave's 20s were spent as a top-rated radio personality in Portland, Ore., at KGW radio. For almost a decade he maintained the highest ratings in afternoon drive time. At age 30, he moved into broadcast television as host and producer of the highly successful and nationally syndicated *PM Magazine*. For the next decade he traveled the world and interviewed famous people for the daily show based in San Diego.

The show offered the opportunity to do some rather unusual things: a mile-high sky diving free-fall, whitewater rafting, and walking on the upper wing of an antique biplane while it flew stunts over the plains of Oklahoma. An avid scuba diver, Dave shot stories under five of the world's major oceans. And he did it all in the interest of keeping the audience compelled to watch. "In broadcast television, especially on a daily show, you have to grab them at the beginning and then keep them for half an hour, he says It's a matter of life and death for your program… We managed to keep *PM Magazine* compelling for 15 years. I try to bring that experience to everything I do. Maybe that has something to do with why our children's movies work so well."

Dave started his production company in 1987 while still hosting *PM Magazine*. He shot commercials on the weekends and in his spare time. He produced more than 70 projects over a three-year period. In 1990, when *PM* left the air (after more than 15 years in syndication), Dave left San Diego for Hollywood, where he studied acting at the respected Charles Conrad studio in Burbank. At the same time, he was producing stories for and appearing on the Discovery Channel's *Tourific Destinations*, once again traveling the world from the beaches of the South Pacific to the castles of Spain.

Eventually, Dave decided that he had traveled enough and began to look for something new and challenging for his entertainment company to produce. The idea for live-action children's movies was born.

Dave's long and distinguished career in entertainment would not have been possible if he had not been able to find a purpose to his life, develop his *own* custom-designed compass, and balance his own needs with the sometimes conflicting needs of others – the very definition of integrity. As Elmer G. Letterman put it, "Personality can open doors, but only character can keep them open."

Dave's character has centered on his commitment to entertain children while, at the same time, educating them and modeling positive values. His career aspiration now is to create an extensive library of children's videos, which can be watched for decades to come. As a father and a professional, he was disturbed by the frequent violence in so many animated cartoons and also on MTV; violent images that use shame and humiliation for dominance and control are what children are constantly absorbing as they watch these programs with their older siblings. Dave remembered with fondness and nostalgia the wonderful programs that he watched such as *Sky King* and *Hopalong Cassidy*, and how inspiring and non-injurious these live-action shows had been for him as a kid.

So, Dave and his partner Ken Urman were inspired to create *Real Wheels*, a live-action show about big equipment that explains how and why things work as they do. Dave's approach from the start was to approach children non-injuriously and also as competent beings. The movies are sprinkled with physical humor that makes viewers laugh; the Dave character actually triggers a lot of laughter since he acts like a kid himself and children relate well to him. Dave has the delightful ability to access the childlike spirit within himself at the same time that he is teaching (and actually making understandable) the technicalities about complicated machinery. As Dave's sister says, "Dave has always been energetic and ambitious, but I think the children's series has really been important to him because it gives a higher purpose to his work."

But even Dave was surprised when he began to witness the huge response, in terms of sales, to his movies. And, he was really taken aback when he learned that the movies were being used not just for entertainment but also for inspiration and for healing. "I really never considered the effect that the movies would have on sick children," he says. "We get letters and e-mail every day from parents who have used the movies for soothing upset children. Sunday school teachers are now using the movies to teach about forgiveness; and retreat directors are using them to help people in transition learn to internalize 'Dave's' spirit of 'moving on.' More recently, due to Dr. Munschauer's interest and involvement, these tapes are being used to give *hope* to people in psychotherapy. And the furthest thought from my mind was that my children's movies would be being shown – and explained – at serious academic conferences!"

Because these tapes are being used to give hope to people, the very making of the *Dave* movies has provided validation for Dave's lifelong interest in resilience. Children are glued to Dave's movies. Perhaps this is because growing up provides all sorts of mini-crises on a day-to-day basis. But what is most moving for Dave is that, in some of the larger crises of life, he has been selected frequently by children through the Make-A-Wish Foundation to be their hero.

The biggest wish of Jack Bajau (6 years old, of Toronto) was to meet his longtime hero Firefighter Dave. Jack had a progressive neurological disease called Rasmussen's encephalitis; his dream was to be a fireman along with his hero, Dave. The *North County Times* in San Diego reported that the little boy's motor skills and neurological responses were "livelier" when he actually *saw* his hero. They enjoyed a twinship experience together, walking among fire trucks and ambulances hand in hand, talking to each other like longtime friends. Dave has said, "I can't think of anything more rewarding for someone who has dedicated 10 years of his life to making movies for kids than to be chosen as a Make-A-Wish celebrity guest. It is heartbreaking for me to think of a young child in pain. If my work can give them even a few moments of happiness, then *all* of the work is worthwhile."

And listening to Dave talk, he is clearly grateful for his success and grateful for the parents and the people he has met who have facilitated his growth and given him opportunities. His movies are replete with messages of gratitude. He tells Becky, "You're the best friend a guy could have." Becky says of Dave, "I'll never know a better astronaut than Astronaut Dave. He's the most unselfish person I've ever known." The dynamic duo expresses hearty gratefulness for being able to talk their way into the monster truck competition arena. Dave is grateful for being able to have the opportunity to try conducting a train, try driving a garbage truck, try driving a bus, to be able to enter into the Kennedy Space Center, and on and on.

Psychologists are discovering that of all variables, the *capacity for gratitude* has the highest correlation with happiness in life. And messages of gratitude for opportunities to learn and experience are in all of Dave's movies. And there is plenteous gratitude expressed towards the authority figures who provide these learning experiences. This value of expressing gratitude and thanks is an extremely important message to impart to our children.

Psychologist Dr. Lynn Levo even suggests an exercise of "practicing" gratitude. By this, she does not mean denying that we might have pain, but she urges people to actively take time each day to keep track of what we are grateful for, for example, in a journal. Though we have rituals of mourning, we have few gratitude rituals. These can be moments of celebration that are salutary for all parties – the kinds of moments we vicariously enjoy so frequently in Dave's movies. Optimism researcher and psychologist Dr. Martin Seligman suggests that people creatively design their own rituals of expressing thanks to those who have done well by us. He urges people actively to think of individuals such as parents, friends, teachers, coaches, teammates, bosses, or employees – or our children – who have been kind to us but have rarely or never heard us express our gratitude; and he suggests composing letters to these individuals and mailing them!

So, think about what circle you would draw around your pyramid now – that is, what purpose and values have been guiding your current life? Are you happy with this circle? Is it consonant with your True Self? If you think of your VP (your Vitality Pulse) as a form of Geiger counter, does it speed up with excitement when you contemplate this circle, or does it become erratic and slow down? If you have just gone through a crisis, might you need now to draw a different circle – to have a different purpose?

Remember the words of writer George Eliot,
"It's never too late to be who you might have been."

# CHAPTER 7

## STORIES OF COURAGE AND SURVIVAL

In writing this book with Dave, as I began to immerse myself in the idea of resilience, I began to notice story after story, all serving to confirm and validate the strength and flexibility that is inherent in our shared human condition and the power that can be summoned within us to bounce back from defeat. A contemporary author, Masten (2001), emphasizes that there really isn't anything magical about people who are resilient – they just are able to adapt, grow, and function because their inborn ability to recover has not been squished or impeded.

A flower can be flexible in stem and stalk to recover its direction only if it has been provided with the right nutrients during its period of growth, or when squashed, if it can find the nutrients it needs, so that it can extricate itself from danger and deprivation, to change direction toward food and light. To quote the words of contemporary jazz singer Lizz Wright, during times of trouble we are all "morning glory[s] lost in a tangled vine."

"Bouncing back," also referred to as "self righting" (Michael Lutter, 1997), has many individual variations. In the face of adversity, people creatively use a wide variety of mechanisms to maintain or restore their self-esteem and feelings of self-efficacy. Dave and I wanted to share some human stories with you to illustrate this variety and to show how much resilience implicitly involves people's knowing how to get their psychological nutritional needs met.

Somehow humans instinctively find the flexibility and capacity to use the environment around them to nourish themselves. This ability to heal and to move on in a successful life often involves the ability to shake off shame feelings, to forgive others, to shed grievances, and to forgive oneself. Often it involves even "forgiving" life for challenging or even catastrophic events and finding the ability still to grow and thrive.

I am grateful to the many people who so graciously and generously shared with us their stories of adversity and triumph. I also hold much compassion for those I approached who chose not to share their stories. We all have had experience with wonderful individuals who are clearly thriving, but who have had terrible life-changing events or have fought in Vietnam or World War II, but who choose to keep the details of their experiences private even from their closest friends and family. These people must be respected as much as those who openly share their stories.

## Weathering the Storm

### Some Public Stories

One of the public places people share their stories is in *Parade* magazine. In August 2003, there was a story of Steven Bishop, who was a successful data sales manager focusing on achieving the American Dream when he was diagnosed with Lou Gehrig's disease or ALS, a degenerative disease of the neuromuscular system, often leading to paralysis and death in two to five years.

His wife, Jennifer, said, "After our diagnosis, our old lives and our old dreams needed to be laid to rest, and we had to decide what our new dreams would be." Steven said, "I never asked, 'What do I need?' Instead I decided to ask, 'What is the most meaningful way we can spend whatever time I have left?'" They decided to dedicate themselves to raising awareness about ALS by speaking in public and sharing their belief that people can live fully, even though their lives are foreshortened.

In the same issue of *Parade*, there was an article about poet Mattie Stepanek, age 13, who has been living with a rare life-threatening disease called mitochondrial myopathy. Mattie has become a best-selling poet whose "heart song books" have inspired millions. *Parade* reported that he also helped a 15-year-old singing star, Billy Gilman (the Muscular Dystrophy Association national youth chairman), to adapt Mattie's poems for Billy's album. And Mattie has joined former President Jimmy Carter in interviewing peacemakers around the world for a new book. To quote Mattie, "This isn't just a 'boo hoo pity me' story. Real kids like me are dying, and we need money for research so we can keep our spirits up on the road to a cure. I may not live to see a cure, but I want to help other kids live way past 13."

Many people, in order to "self-right" or "bounce back," devote themselves to the very painful issues that made them vulnerable in the first place. They engage with the very threat with which they currently have to deal, or have had to deal. A dear friend and colleague of mine, psychoanalyst Dr. Phyllis DiAmbrosio, says, "Just as a biological immunization results from exposure to a noxious

173

substance through vaccination, so too, psychologically, protection lies not in the evasion of the risk, but the successful engagement with it. Resilience proceeds from the adaptive changes that follow from this type of successful coping."

Certainly we can see this "engagement with the risk" in the life of Christopher Reeve, who was injured eight years ago in a horseback riding accident and paralyzed from the neck down, unable to breathe without mechanical help. Because of his determination, he gained some movement and could breathe unassisted for about 90 minutes. In an interview in *USAirways Attaché*, August 2003, Reeve called himself "not a man of optimism, but a man of hope." He also wrote a book titled *Nothing Is Impossible*.

In the article, Reeve says, "No matter what the situation, get busy and find a solution." He says that a lot of people are paralyzed by fear and anxiety instead of being aware of what they can do. By this he means activism. Reeve has been a leading voice on stem cell research and spinal cord injury. He writes, gives speeches, acts and directs. The author of the article in *Attaché*, Diane Cyr, reports that he has a sheet of paper posted on the wall of his specially equipped exercise bike room that says, "For everyone who thought I couldn't do it, for everyone who thought I shouldn't do it, for everyone who said 'It's impossible,' see you at the finish line!" As American lyricist Oscar Hammerstein II said:

"There is a very real relationship, both quantitatively, and qualitatively,
between what you contribute and what you get out of this world."

Reformation: Convict Bo Don Cox

And here is another amazing story about transformation and resilience that came across my desk recently. It is more graphic than most. I can only assume it's true:

I received a letter from a person named Bo Don Cox from Cincinnati, who confessed in the first few paragraphs...

"As you may know, I made a big mistake the night of July 26, 1986. I got into a fight with a young man, walked away, had second thoughts about losing face with my friends, went back, grabbed a baseball bat as I got out of my truck, and hit him in the head. Until recently, I was in prison, serving a life sentence for murder. During my time in prison, I learned a great deal about life, about love, about people, about forgiveness, about redemption, and about the grace of God. I also learned about getting a second chance."

He continues,

"Turning to writing was serendipitous. I started writing for the prison newspaper because a man I looked up to, and was in treatment with, was the editor. Despite the fact that I had no formal training aside from

two English composition classes in my very
brief, amphetamine-laced college career, he
gave me a chance. I began covering prison
events and writing stories. Somehow, I won
two awards for my stories. One was from the
Society of Professional Journalists."

Bo Don Cox goes on to describe how he began writing
meditations in a book called *God Is Not in the Thesaurus*. He says,
"I am starting to realize my writing is a gift, and because of this gift,
I can be a giver rather than a taker. Most of my life I have been a
taker, but now I have a deep need to give back and to help others."
He talks about wanting to give people around the world words of
inspiration and hope, to give people a "new life." He says, "Mine is
the life that has been changed."

Now, he is a regular contributor to *Forward Day by Day*, a
publication devoted to giving people hope who are in all sorts of
disheartening predicaments. He adds:

"The response from many readers helped
to sustain me. Many persons have told me
that God forgives me, that you forgive me.
More times than I can recall, your words
have left me in tears. Through your letters I
have been given a second chance. One letter
that stands out in my mind was from a lady in
Louisiana who said that when she heard I was

a prisoner serving a life sentence in Oklahoma, she thought the folks at Forward Movement lost their 'ever-lovin' minds.' She said her husband, who was an English professor at Tulane, told her to read my meditations before she passed judgment. Fortunately for me, she kept an open mind. Today, she and her husband are two of my best friends. He works with me to improve my poetry, and they both have become involved with prison ministry. Another chance."


## Someone to Watch Over Me

DiAmbrosio has also said that often people are able to bounce back because they are able to find a "surrogate mentor." This can be a person such as a spouse, friend or parent who provides caring and guidance, or it can be an abstract presence held in one's heart, such as God or spirituality.

In terms of the latter, I have a patient in my practice who was called away from his wife and four children when his army reserve unit was summoned and stationed for six months at ground zero after the Sept. 11, 2001, World Trade Center attack. His job was to work with rescue dogs to unearth and identify body parts, scraps of clothing, jewelry and other identifiable objects. He received many awards and honors – even from Mayor Rudolph W. Giuliani and President George W. Bush. To the outside world, it seemed that he should be brimming with pride and feelings of accomplishment.

But unknown even to his wife, he began spending more and more time at gambling casinos. After winning $100,000 on one slot machine pull, he was hooked. He continued to gamble until he had lost his family's car, house, and their vacation cottage. He came to me suffocating in feelings of shame for which he saw no exit but suicide. As we worked together, it became clear that he had been turning to gambling as an antidote for the understandable feelings of helplessness he felt at being confronted daily with death and destruction. He cried, "If I see one more box of Kleenex with people crying, I'll explode."

He wept as he relived with me the seemingly unending days of his close-up experience of the stench in the air, the tears in people's eyes, and his continued feelings of impotence and helplessness. Maybe if he went to the casino, he thought, and at least pulled the right lever at the right time, he could feel some power. Just walking in the door gave him a surge of potential strength, and the high-spirited atmosphere blocked out the darkness in his soul.

As we continued working together, he unearthed more layers of his grief and sorrow about the scenes he had witnessed at ground zero. He became more and more consciously in touch with his anger and frustration at having been able to "do so little to help," and "to be able to do so little to be able to find or rescue life." He began to respect his need to *do* something, but gradually realized that "doing" gambling was only going to destroy him.

His eventual transformation occurred when he realized that he could study to become a pastoral counselor and to help people spiritually with their grieving process. He got spiritual guidance for himself and began pastoral counseling training with a concentration on helping the bereaved.  His goal was to devote his life to helping people with life transitions or grief, so that they could avoid going down self-destructive paths as he did.  Once she understood the dynamics involved, his wife was supportive and agreed to work full time to free him to complete his studies.

## The Hardiness of Hope
## Hunter, Jill & Jim Kelly

*USA Today* announced the story in a full-page spread on the sports page: The only son of Pro Football Hall of Famer and Former Buffalo Bills quarterback Jim Kelly and his wife, Jill, was born with a very rare medical condition called Krabbe (crab a) disease. Compassion for this highly regarded sports figure, beloved by his fans and his city, prompted the nation to respond. Thousands of letters, e-mails and donations poured into the Kelly household.

In the meantime, the Kelly family steeled themselves to try to absorb what seemed to be a blow from life that could not be endured. The perfect picture: handsome, successful sports figure, beautiful wife, bubbly 2-year-old little girl, and now an only son, born on his father's birthday, Valentine's Day, sacked with a disease few had even heard of.  This child bore the name Hunter, a name selected by his father to embody the hope and confidence that his son would follow in his father's footsteps – being strong, powerful and able to tackle anything that came his way.

The doctors' predictions were ominous.  Globoid cell leukodystrophy, more commonly known as Krabbe disease, is an inherited neurodegenerative lysosomal enzyme disorder affecting the central and peripheral nervous systems. Children who inherit the disorder lack an important enzyme (GALC) that is needed for the production of normal myelin (white matter) in the central and peripheral nervous systems. Myelin is the protective covering of the nerve cells and acts like insulation surrounding an electric wire. When the enzyme GALC is deficient it produces toxic substances in the brain, causing myelin loss, change to brain cells, and neurological damage. Progression of the disorder is rapid and death occurs in early childhood. The Kelly family was hit with the somber prognosis that the child, invested with dreams of such a shining future, would have only two years to live.

When I spoke with Jill Kelly, I was moved by the sense of peace and internal strength that I felt emanating from within her. She had a steady and soft-spoken voice indicating that she was mastering very deep feelings, and she told me in detail about the journey that she and her whole family had traversed with Hunter, now 7 years old.

> "My hopes and dreams of having the perfect family were totally shredded and stolen. It was devastating to watch our son struggle. There were so many layers, emotions, questions… so much fear and anger. At times I wondered, 'How can I live anymore?'" Jill told me.

She could find no tangible comfort or consolation within the structured religious denomination in which she was raised, or even in venting and expressing feelings of anger. The sense of helplessness was enormous, especially for Jim, a paragon of physical competence, who could "always make things happen, always fix things, who always had a winner mentality."

Jill felt intense conflict as she grappled with how to spend her time. Should she grieve constantly, and just stare at and hold Hunter? Should she resent people who did not just stop living their lives and stare at him too, since all knew he would be on this earth for only a short while? The Kellys were a visible and popular couple. Some friends remained present, and others drifted away. The couple had to deal with the realization that as they became more confined at home and had less freedom to go out and socialize, some "friends" were less interested in maintaining contact.

Jill's mother was never more than a heartbeat away. When she found out about Hunter's illness she told Jill, "This is a no-brainer, I need to be where I need to be" and gave up her own high-profile career to be free to help Jill. Jill's uncle also rallied to the cause. He had experienced, firsthand, many personal tragedies throughout his own life and made himself available to help Jill grow and find her own spirituality. Specifically, he helped her to be able to reframe Hunter's suffering within the Christian biblical tradition of Christ's own sacrifice out of his love for mankind. Finding this meaning imbued the entire family with a new dedication and commitment to educating themselves further about the Scriptures. Through prayer and reflection, and years of deep contemplation, the Kelly family was able to find a purpose for the suffering they had endured. Jill put it this way: "God gave me my only son to bring me to his only Son."

The family also redefined their own purpose and direction. They wanted Hunter to be an inspiration to others and a story of love. Jill and Jim realized that Jim, because of his renown as a sports figure and because of his popularity, had a huge opportunity to make a difference for other children with the same disease. They wanted to be able to look beyond the pain and tragedy of Hunter's illness, and so they established a foundation called "Hunters Hope" for the purpose of research and education about Krabbe disease. In addition to collecting donations to progress successful treatment of this rare disease, Jill said that their ultimate hope is to prompt people to re-evaluate how and where they spend their time. Hunter was expected to live only until the age of 2, and he is now 7. He has become "our little hero." The Kelly family wants people to see his greatness, how he has "bounced back" time and time again, when he has reached the edge and nobody thought he would survive. Jill told me that "Yes, the foundation needs money, but we are asking people to recognize the bigger picture. We are asking them to change from the inside out. We don't just want you to give monetarily to the foundation and forget about things; we want you to think about how valuable your children are."

Although I have never met him personally, Hunter has become an icon to me. People listen for medical news about him, people talk about him, people on the streets grieve when he goes into the hospital and are gleeful when he "bounces back when no one thought he could." People who have never personally known the Kelly family have experienced the roller coaster of ups and downs for seven years with them. Hunter is hardy, and so is hope.

## Healthy Suppression of Feeling

And many people are resilient because, despite being mistreated, they are able to hold on to a positive view of themselves. For some reason, perhaps due to a special relationship with a grandparent, an aunt or uncle, or a family friend, they do not look for a personal reason to account for the bad things that happen to them. If there has been mistreatment because of dysfunction in their family, they don't take the blame and don't think that the dysfunction is their fault.

I once talked to a woman whose alcoholic father physically abused her mother. She also had a brother who ridiculed and tormented her. Her mother would never stick up for herself, or for her children, and she allowed the father to beat her up and the brother to be nasty to her daughter. This woman was remarkably successful in both her personal and professional life. I asked her, "How did you do it?" She said, "I coped by editing out all the junk – I edited out the dysfunction!" She was able healthily to suppress negative feelings about what was going on around her and to move in her own direction.

She said, "There were terrible crises, there were totally crazy situations. But I always knew they were not my fault. I knew it was not my fault that my father drank and beat up my mother. I was able to do my homework, go to school, entertain myself, and I knew the whole thing wasn't my fault. Even though I had no support or nurturance, I just used the skills I had as much as possible. Of course, I could have done much better if I had support or interest from my parents, but I never thought it was my fault."

## Turn to the Banquet of Nutrients

Rabbi Dennis Shulman

I have also had the privilege of knowing an extremely well-respected psychoanalyst who, at age 53, also became a rabbi. He has published books and articles on biblical psychoanalysis, along with conducting both a busy clinical practice in psychoanalysis and a busy teaching schedule in a prestigious psychoanalytic training center. If this weren't remarkable enough, rabbi, and Dr., Dennis Shulman had gone through almost all of his schooling since childhood completely blind because of a benign brain tumor that he had had since childhood, but was only recently diagnosed. By the time he was an undergraduate at Brandeis University, he had lost his sight completely.

Dennis was open about letting me into his rich internal world. He shared with me the process that enabled him to flourish and enjoy a very full life – interpersonally, spiritually, as a husband and a parent, and now in two careers that he is creatively blending in work and in his publications.

I told Dr. Shulman my experience – that many, obviously successful, people who have physical disabilities had not been willing to be interviewed by me and I wondered why. I found his response to be very interesting. He said that he had observed that many people who had been resilient and had succeeded (in politics, for example, despite being paralyzed, or in music, despite being crippled, deaf, or blind) wanted to remember only their success and therefore resisted revisiting their defeat or their injury.

He also pointed out that even though people externally may look resilient, you cannot really tell whether they *feel* resilient internally. And he noted that there has been so much emphasis on the opposite extremes of either loss and defeat or success that we, as a culture, have not honored resilience, so that even people who have been resilient don't acknowledge it as much as they should.

As both a psychoanalyst and a resilient person, Dr. Shulman was delighted that Dave and I were writing this book as a way of starting to help the public honor resilience as a virtue or attribute. As we talked, I began to see how he had used his initiative to find nourishment for himself as his disability progressed. The initiatives he had taken in growing up and in getting through college going through graduate school, beginning to teach and to publish, learning to refine and develop his ideas, as a blind young person, all reflected intuitively the ideas of the Psychological Nutrition Pyramid.

Dr. Shulman came from Worcester, Mass., a community-oriented small city. He grew up in a Jewish community, which he described as "tight." Many families had moved from Europe, and there were many people with intergenerational connections – many grandparents, parents and friends, all living near each other with close, warm relations. This Jewish community, which was about 10,000 people out of the Worcester population of 200,000, "watched out for me. I never felt teased, and I was never made fun of. It was a very loving community."

As Dr. Shulman described memories of his community, aspects of connectedness and affirmation were in abundance. He remembered being blind and trying to ride a bike, when suddenly two friends showed up "out of the blue," having put layers of foam insulation on their bikes, and offered the bikes to him so he could ride. Should he fall down, the foam would cushion any blow! He also received a lot of affirmation because he was good at music and played drums in a band at teen parties.

There were also many people in his community whom he idealized and could talk to about his religious ideas. They liked to spend time with him helping him develop his ideas, while also providing the opportunity for him to "spar." In all his schools, Dr. Shulman was always able to find male teachers to idealize, and with whom he could have a lively and intensive exchange of ideas about politics, sociology or psychology. He reports having long, intense discussions with his psychology adviser over dinners or by phone – conversations that were, and continue to be, vitalizing to him.

Finally, many of Dr. Shulman's friends still provide continued twinship experiences for him. Six of "the boys" still go away together every summer.

Dennis said that sometimes, when people fuss over him or assume that he needs help, it activates leftover feelings of incompetence that usually lie dormant. He deals with these vulnerable feelings by immersing himself in connectedness. His relationship with his wife and children reminds him of his worth, his lovableness, and his strength.

And in terms of the bedrock need for connectedness, it is

fascinating to hear Dr. Shulman describe the forces that drew him to become a rabbi in his 50s. He said that he felt that religion puts more of an emphasis on the interpersonal and multigenerational context of life than many psychoanalysts do when they focus so intensely on the individual. In fact, Dennis attributes the Worcester community, with its close interpersonal connectiveness, as a big reason he has been able to transcend his disability. As Dave and I would characterize it, he was fortunate to receive in Worcester the nourishment he needed to make his talents thrive and his dreams come true. It is mostly connectedness with other people that has also given Dr. Shulman the resilience to become so successful, widely respected and loved by his colleagues. In fact, it is our connectedness – both past and present – that is the foam on our bicycles that cushions all of us from life's blows.

In terms of Rabbi Dr. Shulman, it is both his intellectual and emotional knowledge of connectedness that led him into rabbinical studies, where he is now teaching others the human nature of interdependence that he began learning at such a young age in Worcester.

## Healing Through Creativity

### Susan Nusbaum

My friend Sue in her 60s, had lost her husband to bladder and liver cancer. They had been married for 40 years and had had a dynamic relationship that was warm and affectionate. She described him as a "life generating source" for her, upon whom she depended for her energy. His varied interests expanded and opened worlds to her, and when he died, the whole structure of her future was disturbed.

Chemotherapy gave the couple and their adult children four months to be together, to complete some furniture making projects (his hobby) and for all to express their feelings to each other. "Right up until the end, he wanted to live," she said. Clearly this was a wonderful marriage for her and a huge loss.

I see her now and she is visibly vital and productive, two years later. I ask how she survived. She told me about her philosophy that "everyone has to have a backup plan." She said that she had been a music major in college and that she had always wanted to do more writing. So, when she found herself flooded with emotions, she wrote.

The loving support that she had had during childhood from her parents, whom she described as "optimistic, loving and always looking on the bright side," gave her the confidence to try to start writing poetry. She said, "I *made* myself do it. I made myself sit down every morning on a schedule and write it, no matter what. I made myself structure every day. I made myself write, and I made myself go out with people." She told me how she would well up with feeling as she tried to weave through her husband's possessions.

Summoning her creative energies gave her a purpose and a diversion. She wrote also about her envy of other couples' intimacy, and she wrote poems about her connections with many other important people in her life. She started to appreciate more and more the value of being alive and having people in close connection with her. She described to me how she drew strength from the huge support system of people who "came out of the woodwork"

– friends, acquaintances, family, some of whom she was not close to before, but who have become dear to her since her husband's death. These feelings of connectedness and purpose sustain her now.

Often, Sue says, the hardest times are when she realizes she cannot share special moments with her husband. For example, she told me that she was riding in the car listening to some beautiful music – so beautiful that she had to pull off the road. In the past, this would be a time when she spontaneously would call her husband at work and ask him to stop what he was doing and tune in to the radio station. But this time she pulled off the road with tears in her eyes, feeling that "I have no one to share this with."

That very evening, she attended a concert with a couple who had been their longtime friends. Kathy said to Sue, "Oh, you won't believe what happened today; I was driving along in the car, and I heard the most beautiful piece of music by Ravel." Sue felt she had heard a voice from heaven! She suddenly realized that although she could no longer share this sort of moment directly with her husband, she did have other very alive connections on whom she could rely.

This realization felt like "almost a religious experience." We can see how, for Sue, the shared appreciation of the music was a link both with the loved person who had passed on, but with one who was very much still alive and "with" Sue in all sorts of meaningful ways. Sue continued: "I loved my life before my husband died, and I continue to love it. Losing him was terrible. I miss him every day, but I have connections and a purpose, and I feel his presence when I think about how I would share things with him, too."

Our thanks to Sue for giving us permission to share this previously unpublished poem:

<u>Found Objects</u>

I found your sailing hat in a drawer,
gray hair stuck in the band
where it grazed your neck.
Squinting, you check the wind
and turn the wheel to fill the sail.


I found your watch glinting
Sunlight on your suntanned wrist,
hand broad-knuckled
on tiller, sand, rake,
on my arm, my lap.


Plans found on your workbench,
neatly measured, drawn and folded -
you show me the angle of the legs,
guiding my hand over the grain
when I bring lunch.


A razor rests
on a bathroom shelf.
Smiling through the steam-fogged mirror,
you stroke your cheeks,

satisfied at their smoothness.


I took your camera to the glacier

and found your shadow,

brilliant blue,

through the lens.

How could I think these objects might

contain your presence,

when I alone am guardian

of your longing to remain.


Susan Dworski Nusbaum, June 2000


## Gratitude & Interdependence

### Laura

Laura suffered both a "life shouldn't have done that," and a "you shouldn't have done that" experience at the same time. Actually, hers was a situation where *many* of life's "shouldn't have done thats" all came together at the same time. When her husband was diagnosed with colon cancer, doctors realized that it was a very unusual form of the disease called familial polyposis. Genetic studies on her children revealed that two of her children had inherited the disease, and her 12-year-old daughter had to have major surgery on her colon as a preventive measure.

At the same time that Laura was dealing with both of these illnesses, a dear friend of hers also contracted a fatal disease and asked her to come and visit. On his deathbed, she saw him miserable, unhappy, suffering with "layers and layers of unresolved issues, bitter, resentful, preoccupied with all the people he didn't like."

Witnessing this man dying with such bitterness gave Laura a flash of insight that "there had to be a better way of dealing with life-and-death crises." Faced with issues of mortality, she realized that she was responsible not only for her husband's future, but even more, for her two children who had inherited the gene for colon cancer. She said, "I *had* to find a good attitude to get them through. I wanted them to go on to lead a healthy and positive life, not to be embittered and negative."

At the same time that Laura's husband was sick and her daughter was having extensive intensive surgery, another (her closest) friend was diagnosed with breast cancer. As if that were not enough, her sister-in-law was dying of skin cancer. Laura said, "It was at that time that I realized, for the first time, that you can't do everything by yourself. When you are humbled by life, you realize that it's better to accept help from people. When everything is good and happy, and you're making a lot of money, you can afford to think, 'I don't like you; I don't like you; I don't like you'; but when you face mortality, or you find yourself in a terrible crisis, you realize that you can't get through it alone. You develop, somehow, a sixth sense about what people are like. People who were there before are not there for you, and people who you never thought would be there, are. Also, as you meet people, you know almost instinctively whether they are true friends or whether they are just going to make you part of their dinner conversation.

"It is humbling to realize how much we need other people. I

was blessed to have a great brother and a wonderful friend who had a positive attitude and was very loving. You have to realize that things happen in life. When you talk to anyone, something has happened to everyone. I can't think of anyone I admire more than my daughter, who had her big surgery at 12. Her own compassion for people is incredible.

"But I feel sorry for her father. Although his own cancer is in remission, he is still negative and is unable to be grateful for all the love and support of those around him. What gets you through trauma is the ability to stop and think about all the people around you – all the *real* people. You can only feel so bad for so long, and then you have to get proactive, or it will all eat you up.

"Despite having lost four people close to her, my oldest daughter loves life and is graduating now from college. She lives every day to its fullest. Maybe if everyone faced their mortality, they would be more appreciative of their life. People have the idea that we should have no disappointments in life and no heartaches, but going through life, with its good and bad, is your history; it's what makes you who you are."

I then asked Laura how she could forgive her husband for continuing to cloud their environment by being so negative when she was trying, so very hard, to provide a positive environment for the children. She said, "Well, I have three great kids. I can forgive him because I'm grateful. I don't want to be an angry person. I just accept the fact that people do stupid stuff. We need to learn from our experience, and if it isn't right, to move on. My philosophy is, you give three chances, and then you move on."

## Take Charge – Be Active

<u>Leon</u>

I also interviewed Leon, whose challenge was to survive and to flourish despite very harsh "*you* shouldn't have done that" experience. He was born to an extremely wealthy family in Germany that owned a large bank. They escaped from the Nazis when he was 4 years old, but they were allowed to bring no money with them to the United States. Only his parents, his brother, he, and his nanny could come.

When he related this story of horror to me, his first response was that "The Nazi invasion never affected me, other than the fact that we moved to the United States." Recognizing the discrepancy between his own subjective experience and the Nazi horror story, I inquired further about what elements were in place in his life at that time that softened such a horrific event. He told me at length about the loving, close family he had and the richness of his emotional support. His faithful nanny stayed with him until he was 16 and lived until he was 69 years old. Though his parents discovered that his sister had been killed at Auschwitz, they turned their attention from that tragedy and toward mastering the challenges that came with their new lives in the United States.

Unlike many refugees, Leon's family made it their mission to learn to speak English immediately, which led to his father's finding a job as an interpreter. Both parents became active in Jewish organizations and in societies that backed the arts. Leon absorbed his parents' dedication to activity and to work, and insisted on paying for his own schooling. Early on he took on a paper route and worked in a steel plant. He became committed to achievement and cultivated a strong work ethic. He learned how to manage his time, committed himself to achievement, and incorporated the value of activity over passivity. He discovered that if he programmed and structured his time well, he could be a success.

The culmination of Leon's success came with the ownership of a large company that won many awards and made millions of dollars in profit over the years. Unfortunately, this company had very difficult and dissatisfied union leaders who spearheaded a strike that ultimately shut down the company. Leon suffered a huge financial loss to both his business and personal assets. He told me that union bosses threatened the lives of his wife and children, slashed company managers' tires, damaged expensive company equipment, and damaged the electrical systems in the manufacturing plant and their homes.

But Leon used activity, and his commitment to competency and effectiveness, to get him through. He had always liked being "in movement" and in motion – the same mechanisms his father used when he "hit the ground running" at Ellis Island. "What keeps me going is feeling that nothing can get me down," Leon told me. "I've had to learn to be good at putting adversity somewhere in the back of my brain and to move forward. I have no patience after a while with people who linger in a bad event. Life dictates that you move on."

## Tend, Befriend and Create

### The Gelbs

Joan and Victor Gelb faced one of the most devastating "life shouldn't have done thats" when they lost their 43-year-old son, Bobby, to AIDS. As they watched his body disintegrate and barely survive infections such as pneumonia, the family mobilized around him like wagons circling a camp. When he was ill, one of the siblings was always with their parents, and the Gelbs say they survived this chronic stress because of the support and presence of their "wonderful friends." Joan said, "I don't know what we would have done without them. We have a close network of friends – five couples that have been friends of ours for 50 years. They are like family. Just their being there helped us get through."

In addition, the family style was to be aware of and openly express feelings. They did this with each other and with their son in both a physical and verbal manner. There was a lot of hugging and kissing, and many good talks. There was open discussion about death and therefore no unfinished business. At Bobby's death, everyone "was at peace" and there were no unanswered questions.

Bobby was never afraid of dying, only worried about how his parents would endure their pain. His compassion for others had come to the forefront, as had his own activism. Bobby did more to promote AIDS awareness in his community than anyone else had ever done. He gave interviews about AIDS prevention and left a legacy of courage in living with AIDS. Efforts were made to educate the Jewish community about AIDS and the attitude that there should be no shame or embarrassment associated with the disease.

At Bobby's funeral, a thousand people attended and everyone wore a red ribbon recognizing the AIDS organization.

Bobby's father, Victor, also continued to be active in education about prevention. He became chairman of the Citizens Committee on HIV and AIDS, appointed by the mayor of Cleveland, the county commissioners, the Gund Foundation, the Cleveland Foundation, and the United Way. Within three months after Bobby died, this commission issued a report of 21 recommendations that have become the blueprint for HIV education in Cleveland. In addition, both Joan and Vic Gelb have now for many years been honorary chairs of the AIDS Walk that has become the largest fund-raising effort for the local AIDS organization.

Through the Gelbs' work, they have actively dealt with the issue of AIDS and a real "life shouldn't have done that" experience. Their attitude is "Move on if you can; just don't go backward." They have also actively dealt with any possible discriminatory issues towards homosexuals (or "*you* shouldn't have done that" issues) by contributing their energy to helping reconcile attitudes about biblical prohibitions. They have shared their experience and wisdom in both the Jewish and general communities. All this work has had the salutary effect of helping to heal their own wounds as well as the potential wounds of others.

### Twinship: *The Sisterhood of Survival*
By Gene Warner

~ Reprinted by permission of *The Buffalo News*. Originally published on Oct. 29, 2003

Patty Gelman was at a party last fall when she met a fellow breast cancer survivor, a woman still going through chemotherapy. Someone brought the two women together – one with short hair, the other with a wig – introducing them by their first names. They chatted about the dark days of chemotherapy, and finally something Gelman said prompted the other woman to say, "I know somebody you should talk to – Petty Gelman." "I am Patty Gelman," she replied. The two women had never met. But they had talked on the phone several times.

Their conversation was the product of the often-informal network of breast cancer survivors. The other woman had been given Gelman's name when she needed to talk with someone who had gone through chemo. This network – perhaps there are several networks – includes hundreds if not thousands of local [Buffalo] women.

Through e-mails, telephone lifelines, support groups and other means, breast cancer survivors have banded together to battle the disease, which strikes more than 1,250 Western New York women each year.

They call themselves survivors, not victims. And they tackle the illness head-on, shrugging off any stigma of cancer and reaching out to help each other. Their network operates in many ways. Gelman wrote a book about it, from the e-mails she sent friends and loved ones during her year-long journey through Cancer World; Miriam C. Dow helped set up a video series for women diagnosed with breast cancer that has been distributed to medical centers in 48 states and six nations; Bertha M. Hill organized a local chapter of the Sisters

Network, mostly African-American breast cancer survivors; and Susan G. Wood is a charter member of Hope Chest, a paddling team of breast cancer survivors. They've battled to exert their will over the disease, rather than let the disease control them.

This networking activism helps these women inoculate themselves against depression – the feeling you get when you feel trapped, overwhelmed and alone.

"What you do is inspire each other, empower each other and give each other, the courage to move on with your life and not give up," said Kenneth N. Condrell, a local family therapist. "Having a support group when you're overwhelmed is unbelievably therapeutic."

Hill put it another way: "I look at us as being soldiers, and there are a lot of one-breasted warriors out there."

After Gelman was diagnosed with breast cancer early last year, she didn't want to see many people or sound like a broken record on the phone. So the Snyder woman vented her feelings the modern way, via e-mail, often in the middle of the night when sleep proved elusive.

Her e-mails tell the human side of her yearlong roller-coaster ride through diagnosis, surgery, chemotherapy and radiation to attack her breast cancer.

They're filled with honesty, laughs, insights into the treatment and drug therapy decisions she faced, and self-deprecating jabs at herself, especially her bald head and wig.

Gelman realized she was doing more than venting her emotions. "Gradually I realized that my e-mails were doing more than communicating with friends and family, and sustaining and entertaining me," she said. "When I realized that the e-mails were being circulated beyond my personal network, it occurred to me that others might benefit from reading my story."

So those e-mails have become a book called *Humor After the Tumor*, with proceeds going to Roswell Park Cancer Institute, in Buffalo.

Even the title suggests something about the way women now react to breast cancer. They're not afraid to shock others. The word "tumor" appears in Gelman's book title. A group that sponsors breast cancer walks is called Bosom Buddies. An art fund-raiser using brassieres was called Bra-vo. And the dragon-boat paddling team is called Hope Chest. "A generation ago, the whole topic was an embarrassment," Gelman said. "Women were shamed into hiding." No longer...

Miriam Dow of Buffalo already had been diagnosed twice with breast cancer. She felt alone, isolated, in her battle. So five years ago, she attended a meeting that changed her life. About a dozen local women, led by Dr. Lucie DiMaggio, talked about creating a video series, featuring breast cancer survivors who could help teach newly diagnosed women where to turn for help.

Five years later, WomenStories has raised $507,000 and sent 9,000 copies of its six videos to libraries, medical centers and clinics in 48 states and six nations.

"It's a whole new way to give support for any illness," said Dow, executive director of WomenStories. "The survivors are the authorities. The people who have gone through the illness can give the best advice and support."

The six videos already created – on topics ranging from chemotherapy and surgical choices to intimacy and young women with breast cancer – feature local women of various ages and backgrounds giving pointed advice: Don't be afraid to say no to a doctor or seek a second opinion. Be as informed as possible, through research from the Internet and other sources. Talk to other women who've gone through similar treatment.

"Every step of the way, you're given choices," Dow said. "We hope the videos will help women make good choices."

The videos, much like Gelman's book, have one overriding message. "Women want to tell other women: 'You're going to get through this, and most likely you'll be OK. But it's not pleasant,'" Dow said.

Patty Gelman had a plan for her breast cancer, a disease that already had struck her mother, grandmother and maternal aunts. A routine mammogram would reveal a lump; early detection would lead to a double mastectomy and reconstructive surgery. But fate, she writes, had a different plan for her.

On Dec. 25, 2001, she felt a lump in her armpit the size of a large grape. Two and a half weeks later, she learned she had cancer that had spread to at least one lymph node.

Her plan for a double mastectomy hit a snag when Dr. Stephen Edge of Roswell Park Cancer Institute said 20 years of data no longer supported a double mastectomy for her case; because the cancer in her body posed a greater risk of returning than any new cancer, he suggested a lumpectomy, followed by aggressive chemotherapy, radiation and follow-up drugs. That's the course she would steer through her disease.

Gelman's 46 e-mails provide insights into her year with cancer. She tells about "hugging the couch" for the first four days of each chemotherapy cycle; shaving her head as a pre-emptive strike against her hair falling out; the mind-numbing power of anti-nausea drugs; and the supportive role her husband, Warren, three daughters, two siblings and dog played in keeping her as upbeat as possible during the darkest days. But she didn't mince words about the effects of the chemo some days.

Following one tough weekend, Gelman wrote: "For those of you who have been wondering (and worrying) about how I always seem so upbeat, I thought today would be a perfect day to share my feelings of the moment: This sucks."

A year ago September, Gelman had mixed emotions about her radiation treatments coming to an end. Doctors no longer would monitor her so closely; aggressive treatments no longer would attack her disease. "After next month, I think I'll feel more helpless," she wrote. "As happy as I am to notice my eyebrows growing back, they are a clear indication that all that poison is out of my body and not killing cancer cells anymore." Gelman no longer would be attacking her disease so actively, and that hurt.

Six years after being diagnosed with breast cancer, Bertha Hill refuses to let breast cancer define her. "I don't wear a sign," she said. "I don't have any labels on my forehead, and I have a name. It's Bertha Hill, not Breast Cancer."

But Hill saw a need in the African-American community, and she helped fill it by setting up a local chapter of the national organization

Sisters Network. "Our mission is to increase the local and national attention to the devastating impact that breast cancer has in the African-American community," she said.

African-Americans' death rates from breast cancer are 28 percent higher than whites', according to Sisters Network figures. Research suggests the disease is more aggressive in black women; other factors may include a lack of health insurance, later diagnosis, and less knowledge about the disease.

The local Sisters Network chapter – with 25 black women and one white woman – reaches out into the community, taking information about breast cancer into churches, adult education classes, drug rehab programs, jails, and nursing homes. The network also has a monthly support group, promoting sisterhood among breast cancer survivors.

"If we can beat breast cancer, we can overcome anything else," Hill said. "Cancer treatment is not easy. Once you go through cancer treatment, you can deal with the small stuff."

Susan Wood will never forget the moment, in September 2000, when her 22-woman team participated in its first dragon-boat race at Ontario Place.

While the 44-foot boat finished fifth out of six – "first in our lane," Wood quipped – she remembers the rush she felt when the boat crossed the finish line. "I was yahooing," she said. "In an instant, I felt I was back. It was the most alive I had felt since the day I was diagnosed."

Wood is one of the charter members of Hope Chest, a team of breast cancer survivors led by local fitness trainer Laurie Dooley.

A Vancouver doctor, Donald McKenzie, launched the first dragon-boat team in 1996, to challenge the belief that exercise could lead many breast cancer patients to suffer from a condition known as lymphedema.

When she was diagnosed in January 2000, Wood immediately went from feeling like a person who had taken care of her body, who worked out frequently, to a person who was sick, who felt alienated from her body. She felt like a complete outsider. Until the day when her boat crossed the finish line. Breast cancer, she said, can mean a loss of control for women.

"You can't control the physical aspects of the disease and whether it's going to come back," she said. "But you can control how you react to it and how you move forward." Wood, who now coordinates a breast cancer prevention study at Roswell Park, referred to the sisterhood of survivors. "There's a definite connection that occurs," she said of meeting fellow survivors. "It's almost electric. You feel like you've known them forever."

In December, a woman asked Gelman how she could help a neighbor with breast cancer who asked to be alone.

"I remembered feeling helpless when I was on the other side of the situation and convinced her that she should ignore the woman's requests to be left alone," Gelman wrote. "I assured her that as long as she respected her friend's privacy, anything that she did, sent, or left at her door would comfort her friend."

After finishing chemotherapy and radiation, Gelman met a woman just diagnosed with breast cancer who asked what advice she could give her. "My answer to anyone will always be this: Keep your sense of humor; it's not a death sentence. Seek second opinions, and choose a medical team whose priority is your comfort, both emotional and physical."

Dr. Edge, chairman of breast surgery at Roswell Park, gave the second opinion that helped Gelman decide she didn't need a double mastectomy.

After reading her e-mails, he was struck by her strength, by her love of life. "And ultimately, that is what I have learned from all the Pattys that I have served," he said. "People have a remarkable inner strength, a will to live, and an optimism that always conquers the darkness and pain they face. I stand in awe at the resilience and fortitude of people facing these diseases and their treatments."

## Provide Twinship and Teach

### "Squiggy"

I recently interviewed actor David Lander, best known for his character Squiggy on the television sitcom *Laverne & Shirley*. When the disease multiple sclerosis intruded into his life, it was such a shattering "life shouldn't have done that" experience that he kept his illness a secret for 15 years. When he decided to "come out of the closet," *People* magazine featured him in an article titled "Out of Hiding." At that same time, Penny Marshall called him and asked if he would be an honoree at an MS fund-raising event that had previously honored Annette Funicello and Richard Pryor.

I had great empathy with David when I heard that he had kept his disease a secret, for I had been puzzled by my intense feelings about keeping my own breast cancer a secret – a reaction that I never would have predicted I would have. So I asked him more about the secrecy. He said *People* magazine characterized his secret-keeping as courageous, but added, "I don't see courage in hiding."

He added that, although his wife and daughter knew about his diagnosis, he wanted to keep it secret from "show business" because he feared it might limit his opportunities as an actor. He said that he felt shame about the diagnosis, for he was afraid that people would see him as weak or give him "patronizing pats on the back." At the time he was diagnosed, treatments were not as available as they are now. He was put on steroids and told "old wives' tales about bee stings and things." He said, "I hated myself, I wondered whether I could work. I went through periods of anger and denial." I could resonate deeply with his words, for shame is what I felt too about my cancer – shame – a feeling of there being something seriously "wrong with me," or "weak."

When David decided to reveal his illness, he was met by very warm responses. He received a letter saying, "Dear David: I've had MS for 20 years and I hid it for 12 years. I feel much better now. Welcome to the club!" David also noticed that there were no books that dealt with the subject of people who were living (and surviving) with MS. He wanted to write a book that captured day-to-day moods of a person with MS. In almost the same words, he told me what clergyman and writer Edward Everett Hale has said, "I cannot do everything; but I will not let what I cannot do interfere with what I can do."

So David focused his creativity on writing *Fall Down Laughing:*

*How Squiggy Caught Multiple Sclerosis and Didn't Tell Nobody.* He shares the story of his own journey and struggle with MS. In addition, he now travels extensively, giving inspirational speeches on behalf of the MS Society. He accompanies doctors who describe the latest developments in MS research and then talks to groups of patients. It is mingling with the patients that he loves the most – and using his acting talents to make them laugh, as he teaches them about MS and shares his own journey.

Much of what David talks about is the hiding. He describes moments that everyone in the audience can relate to that "were traumatic in the past, but are now funny." As an example, one day he was trying to walk through a park to Union Station in Washington. He asked a friend to hail him a cab – a friend who wasn't aware of his disease. She said to him, "You don't need a car! You can just walk down the steps." Once he began describing to the audience the cobblestone that lay before him, everyone in the audience began rolling their eyes. He told me that "when you talk about cobblestones to healthy people, they just picture a beautiful street. But when you talk about cobblestones to people with MS, everyone knows what you mean – trying to negotiate the stones with a dropped foot, maybe falling on the ground, or rolling along on a wheelchair, feeling like you're in a Mixmaster. It's a story everyone can relate to."

Or, another example is how "everyone giggles when I mention the story that was reported on *60 Minutes*, before we knew what the true therapy was for MS, about fillings in one's teeth being responsible for the disease. Because many people in the room have removed all their metal fillings and have a (needless) small fortune invested now in their gold teeth!"

He also shares with them private feelings that all have experienced but never said out loud, such as "looking at your legs and saying, 'I can't take you out anymore' – being mad at a part of your body for not being able to do something." David described the mutual sharing and warmth he feels with these MS groups. To quote: "It's not me and them, it is us. Here I am around people I would never have known before. We have nothing in common but one thing – but oh, what a thing! People who have just met each other become tremendous support for one another." (What a wonderful description of twinship.)

When we discussed his acting, David said that although his daughter is very excited about her upcoming acting career, he now gets much more gratification from performing in-patient programs than from pursuing his public acting career. "That's where I express my creativity - in the stories I tell and how I relate to people." One person recently said to him, "I can't remember laughing out loud since I've had MS, till I saw you."

David adds: "Making people laugh is sort of like being on *Laverne & Shirley*, or doing a play. I accept the fact that there are so many ways that you can get people turned on. Speaking to patients does have a show business element, but the effect lasts longer." (What a wonderful dose of mirroring and idealization these patients get from David, as well.) He told me that he has also made an audio version of his book for people whose eyes are failing due to MS, and he has heard others say that they play the audio in their cars over and over again to cheer up and to elevate their mood.

To summarize, all these stories are of people who have shown resilience. They have all been able to mobilize themselves and to get nourishment for their basic needs. They have creatively found ways, within the uniqueness of their individual selves and the idiosyncrasies of their environments, to move forward with their lives. They have all intuitively embraced the **P.R.I.D.E. Factor**™ to survive. That is, they have been able to capture, or recapture, Positivity (things can get better), Resilience (life is worth living), Integrity (a focus on what is now valuable to them), Discipline (to move forward), and Enthusiasm (for living).

In addition, they have all been able to discover, or rediscover, a purpose and a direction – often moving forward on a very different course than they ever could have predicted earlier. Their new dreams, since they provide such vitality, can be seen as newly discovered aspects of their own True Selves. This is because our True Selves are surprisingly much more complex and flexible than we might ever know until we are faced with the demands and challenges of a life crisis.

# CHAPTER 8

# USE OF THE DAVE MOVIES TO *HELP* PEOPLE IN REAL LIFE

As Grant and I experienced the soothing effect of the *Dave* movies upon ourselves, and as I began to sort out the messages of health that are conveyed in the subcontext of his movies, it was a very short step for me to begin thinking about how I might be able to use Dave's messages, both in my own life and even in my clinical practice.

First of all, the mantra "shouldn't have done that" inched its way into my style of speaking and to that of my whole family. Then, I found it sneak into my clinical work, and my patients found relief from their shame as they began to use it. For people holding long-standing grudges, we applied the "you shouldn't have done that" phrase to soften feelings of hatred and victimization. Relief sets in as one begins to feel free to move on with life, unencumbered by a burdensome grievance story. Spirits began to lighten. Increasingly, I began to witness the effects of Dave's messages in various situations. Bubbling with enthusiasm, I shared the Dave movies with several of my friends of differing disciplines who were interested in interpersonal relations and in healing.

One of these friends, Rev. Susan VandeKapelle, began using the tapes for her summer retreats at Lake Chautauqua, where she was helping women who were struggling with midlife transitions. Other friends of mine who were also psychoanalysts borrowed the movies to show to their patients who held particularly intractable reactions of shame and guilt. I could see enthusiasm spreading among professional people for whom I had extremely high regard (idealization) suggesting that I was on the right track about my inclination to make *serious* use of these children's tapes in treatment and healing settings.

Because of the healthy messages of child development, Dave and I can see future use for his movies in school settings, religious instruction, and in virtually any other arena in which teaching children about resilience is held as a value. The possibilities ahead are very exciting and inspiring to us.

We look forward to the prospect of having more examples of the active use of Dave's movies to share with you; but for now, we will offer you the following.

The Perfectionist: "Trent"

"My whole life I have had an inborn need for perfection, a drive to constantly strive for the approval of those around me. At first thought, you may think that this type of behavior is normal. Frequently, athletes, entertainers, and others, strive for perfection in their line of work. The difference however, is that my desire for perfection had consumed every aspect of my life, and dictated my every decision. I can tell you, through experience, that a life of perfection is everything but… it's no life at all.

Any actions I would take were carefully planned so that I would avoid conflict with others and also give them the most happiness. This happened regardless of which personal sacrifices I would have to make or pain I would need to endure. I missed out on many life experiences, from my childhood through to my adult years, because of my self-imposed imprisonment in perfection. Even though I was consciously aware of what I was doing, I couldn't prevent it.

After years of undue stress and anxiety over this situation, one night it all ended. Never would I have expected my cure to come from a movie found within the *children's* section of the video store, but indeed it did. I admit that once my psychoanalyst, Dr. Carol Munschauer, first suggested the Dave movies, I was a little hesitant. However, Dr. Munschauer explained the success she had in patients with different conditions. She wouldn't explain how *There Goes a Monster Truck* would help me – she wanted me to discover that myself, and it didn't take long!

There is no doubt that children will love Dave's movies for the lessons he teaches as well as his funny antics, yet he helped cure me. Throughout his movie series, Dave inevitably makes mistakes, blunders and gaffes, that lead to his sometimes disappointing himself and others. But, the most important part of the movies is what happens after his miscues: he is forgiven, learns from his errors and life goes on. No important person leaves Dave's life forever just because of Dave's shortcomings; no one is permanently scarred; Dave just keeps going on.

It seems like such an easy lesson, a quick cure, yet it took me well into adulthood to understand – and all from a 30-minute 'children's' movie. Dave's curative abilities may not be obvious to the casual viewer, but perhaps the subconscious messages are the most effective. If Dave's movies can cure a lifelong problem such as mine in 30 minutes, imagine the tremendous preventative benefit to children who watch his series regularly. Dave has helped, and will continue to help, entire generations to grow both inside and out. Since coming to the realization that perfection is not the only way, and that it's OK to be fallible, my life has changed greatly! The stress I put on myself to please everyone in my life is now greatly diminished. I am now able to make decisions based on my own feelings and values rather than caving in to others' beliefs: having to be perfect.

Even being able to say no once in a while when a friend or family member asks for a favor is a huge step. Before watching Dave's movies, I would never have been able to make these steps towards emotional independence, because I never could have had the permission to be imperfect."

After discussing the above patient with an analyst friend of mine, we focused more closely on the potential use of the Dave movies in psychotherapy for people who couldn't forgive themselves when they fall short of their own unrelentingly high standards. He told me of a patient of his who, despite years of treatment, remained intensely self-critical. This man was a businessman in his early 50s who was oppressed by the inner image of a brilliant father who expected perfection from him, but who was never able to acknowledge his accomplishments. Nothing this man did as a child quite satisfied his father. As a result, the patient developed an obsessive perfectionistic personality, which led him to recurrent, sometimes debilitating, depressions and intense and recurrent feelings of shame when he could not live up to his own ideals or expectations.

My colleague shared with me that this man was a very loving person and deeply wanted to change this part of his personality because he saw it affecting his children, who were also becoming plagued by the tyranny of perfection. So, my colleague decided that he would give his patient *There Goes a Monster Truck* movie to watch with his children. He prefaced this gift by saying that Dave has a way of softening shame experiences by saying, "Shouldn't have done that" when he has made a mistake and then he moves on.

The patient watched the Dave movies for months with his son. After about six months, my colleague, curious about his new, and unusual, approach of using the movies in treatment (and also wanting the tapes back to give to another patient), found a moment in the session to inquire about his patient's reaction to *Monster Truck*. The response was, "I really wanted to study it all on my own to be sure I didn't miss anything. I wanted to take notes and be sure I understood every detail so I didn't miss any nuance – but my kids have totally appropriated that movie and won't let me have it back! They watch it over and over and over and over again!" Well, I guess we can say that the patient's perfectionism isn't cured yet, but maybe the children are getting the healing message.

There Goes a Monster Truck & The Effects of Ground Zero:
Rev. Joseph F. Moreno, A Ground Zero Chaplain

"As I arrived in 'the pit' – the floor of ground zero – on Sept. 11, 2001, at 12:27 p.m., it was a scene of total destruction, chaos, human suffering, and pandemonium. For a few short seconds, I thought this scene was something out of a movie or the television show *ER*. But, the screaming, the yelling, the blood, the tears, the human devastation, the smoke, the fires, the panic of people and emergency services was something that even Hollywood could not produce. The reality of this tragedy was too real – no sound effects or props could ever duplicate it.

"In my seven months of service at ground zero and in my work with families in counseling, I had an experience of transformation. The suffering and the experience of death that touched so many people in such a short period of time transformed caregivers and all those involved to use their skills, their faith, and their human resources to bring hope and calm to the professionals charged with the responsibility of search and rescue and recovery.

"From police officer to firefighter to construction worker to EMT, all of whom were stationed at ground zero – all were concerned with finding life in the World Trade Center towers, helping those in need of medical care, helping those who needed to be emancipated from the crumbling and broken debris of previously strong and daunting structures. It was incredible to see and know that each time one was going in to look for life or death.

"The fire, the smell, the chemicals, the black smoke was so thick and intense, one could not see far. It was like taking baby steps in trying to find people to help. For one woman who was buried under piles of brick and steel beams, it was fate that she was found. She was eating a tuna fish sandwich, and the smell of tuna through the maze of smoke and fire allowed us to find her. She had multiple broken bones and lacerations. It was the first sign of hope after we had looked for 21 hours.

"The core word here is *hope*. A small glimpse of life can become rays of hope for those who are working in a search and rescue operation. The hope is needed to find life, but also the hope is needed for those who have the special calling to work with search and rescue to know that their *own* families are OK and that they themselves have hope.

"In watching the many *Real Wheels* movies, I can see why, after Sept. 11, these videos became exceptionally important for parents and children. For many days after Sept. 11, the general fear in the world was who was next. Would this be the end of the world?

"Fear and panic were taking shape in all phases of life. From governmental officials to religious leaders, to police and fire personnel, all had something in common. The common thread was the goal of bringing peace, calmness and hope to a society and planes full of terror.

"The *Real Wheels* video series offers the child and parent a place of hope and peace. The child's journey of excitement and fantasy with monster trucks, airplanes, fire trucks and bulldozers creates a feeling of happiness. It is OK to be in this space of playing and dreaming with the fire truck, the monster truck, etc.

"With the world 'glued' to television sets watching the events unfold, the child is now in a controlled world with symbols he is used to seeing in books, cartoons and in real life. The fire truck, the plane, the truck and beyond represent a space for the child to feel safe in and secure. No harm will come to him in light of what is taking place in the real world after Sept. 11.

"The videos are happy and full of a child's excitement and energy. Children can see themselves driving the monster truck, the plane, the fire truck, etc. They *become* the main character of the video in wanting to drive and experience all the fun in driving.

"For the parent, having these videos available for their children allows them to influence the development of their child's inner world in healthy and growth-promoting ways. It's OK, we're safe, Mommy and Daddy are safe and OK. The videos project hope, peace and calmness to a child's inner world. Policemen, firefighters and rescue heroes are not just here for tragedies.

"The *Real Wheels* movies are full of messages of redemption. When Dave makes a mistake with the monster truck, he says, 'Oh, I shouldn't have done that.' The observation that it's OK to make mistakes brings a sense of security for the child and even adults. Mistakes are a part of the world order and the process of life.

"Too many times when children and adults make mistakes, feelings of guilt, condemnation, and fear become so great that people can't move beyond their mistakes. In Dave's videos, the child gets the message, over and over, that it's OK to make mistakes, but then it's time to take action, to move on and try harder.

"It is the positive attitude of hope, the flexibility to shed shame, and the encouragement to take active steps to transform one's situation that motivates change and enables 'bouncing back' as Dave and Dr. Munschauer call it. Guilt, negative reinforcement, and fear will never motivate either child or adult to overcome mistakes or to transform experience into a moment of learning, change or wisdom.

"I am a priest, so I see things also from a religious perspective. When Jesus conducted his public ministry, he did not condemn people or judge them. His words of compassion, kindness and serenity were the core of his being. 'Oh, I shouldn't have done that' reflects a compassionate correction and a teaching moment. I see in my ministry now that both children and adults need this.

"Jesus' entire life shows us that when people are able to move beyond a traumatic experience they can become whole again and complete. But when the *mistake* becomes the focus and center of one's life, recovery can be stalemated and one's feeling of low self-esteem and self-worth suffer. This is when symptoms can become entrenched and, as I have witnessed in my work with the police, when acting out even of a suicidal or violent nature, can occur. Dave's movies all give children the permission and freedom to know that mistakes can be made without having to feel judged or blamed for life.

"We used the same principle at ground zero with the search and rescue K-9 division. The dogs were becoming extremely depressed after a week of failing to find any survivors. The dogs would not eat or drink; they were so depressed they couldn't function. Their despair was visible and it affected their owners and trainers.

"So, what was done to help the K-9 core was to assure them that they were loved, and that it was OK that they did not find life. It wasn't their fault. This was achieved by changing their daily routine outside the ground zero setting. It was transforming to see how the positive message of letting the dogs know that they were good and that it was OK that they 'didn't do that' (to paraphrase Dave's mantra) freed both the dogs, and their owners to move on.

"On May 7, 2003, I was called by a former parishioner to come at once to their house. Their daughter, a teenager, was locked in her bedroom threatening to kill herself. Her father and mother were both police officers, and she had broken into their gun cabinet and taken one of their guns.

"When I arrived at the house the fear and panic, of course, was very high. I spoke with the girl by cell phone for about two hours before she allowed me to come in. She was shaking and crying, and wheeling the gun toward her head and mine. We spoke for about an hour. She was very upset. She had done something that, according to her own religious beliefs, would be considered very wrong.

"I noticed while in her room that she had a remote-control Ford monster truck. She told me that she loved big trucks. I shared with her that I happened to have a video in my car that I wanted to watch with her. So, as some trust had been established and things had settled down a bit, we watched *There Goes a Monster Truck*. As she watched I began to see a decrease in her anger towards herself, and her panic began to dissipate.

"I told her that it's OK when we make mistakes, and as in the video, 'Oh, I shouldn't have done that,' we need to learn and grow from our mistakes. As I shared with her, there is life and hope after our mistakes… Within a few hours she gave me the gun, and she told me what she did. My response was, 'It's OK. Oh, you shouldn't have done that,' but you are going to be OK and you need to move on.

"I have been a law enforcement chaplain for many years. I have seen many deaths, accidents, illnesses, suicides and other suffering. The common denominator with life's tragedies is fear and the question of acceptance. Will life ever be OK again? What will happen next? How will I survive?

"In all of the *Real Wheels* movies Dave gives us the wisdom, 'Oh, I shouldn't have done that,' to take life's cycles of good and bad and move on in our world with a renewed sense of hope, a revitalization of ourselves, a sense of happiness and peace.

"I would only make one change to *There Goes a Monster Truck*; it should be for *all* ages, not just ages 3-8.

## CHAPTER 9

## SPECIFIC STRATEGIES TO HELP YOU "BOUNCE BACK"

Dave and I now offer you some specific strategies you can actively use to help you bounce back from a setback or even traumatic event.

Do not isolate yourself from your emotions. Recognize and name the particular disappointment or failure. What "shouldn't have done" has happened? Find specific words for the loss or injury and acknowledge them. As with shame, even the ability to name the feeling is halfway to being able to solve the problem.

Allow yourself to share your feelings with at least one trusted friend in order to begin to grieve and to start the process of working through, or metabolizing, whatever loss has occurred. Is it an "I shouldn't have done that"; a "you shouldn't have done that to me"; or a "life shouldn't have done that to me"? The same principles apply if the loss is a loss of self-esteem or a diminishment in a feeling of competency. *Always* encourage yourself to define and verbalize your emotional state.

Be clear to yourself when you have a shame feeling. Exposing shame feelings to daylight, even just to yourself, makes shame feelings shrivel. This is because shame feelings hate daylight, just as vermin hate daylight.

Break the silence. Try to tell a trusted friend about your feelings. He might be able to help you put them in perspective. If he knows you and your family, he may even be able to shed some light on *how* you developed these shame feelings in the first place. This opens up some space for a more objective (and positive) perspective. Remember, "it's the secrets that kill people. It's the stuff that leads people to alcoholism, drug abuse, broken relationships, loss of jobs, unemployment, and violent behaviors." (Rev. Bruce N. Teague, abuse survivor)

And, be kind to yourself. Realize that with all shame feelings, you may have strong sensitivities so practice ways of trying hard to not allow these sensitivities to be acted upon in unhealthy or destructive ways once they are evoked. Remember that shame is about hurt and anger is merely a camouflage for vulnerability. Practice how to just *feel* ashamed without having to explode in anger or contempt or to reflexively shame someone else in return.

Dave and I believe in *mobilizing* when you have experienced defeat – not right away, but pretty soon. People thrive on the feeling of self-efficacy – the sense that they have the power to overcome their challenges. The process of just getting through a traumatic event can be so painful – or even horrendous.

Initially, the shock and surprise of an event can be so discouraging that you may not be able to see beyond it. Therefore, it is important to allow yourself some time. Realize that it takes space and "down time" to metabolize a loss, to find words for the feelings, to experience and resolve, for example, a depression caused by a traumatic situation. Allow yourself to coast for a while and trust in your own "psychological immune system." Just as the body finds a way to fight off toxins that threaten its welfare, the psyche also mobilizes defenses to soften the impact of negative stressors. These defenses automatically come into action to fight off injury, push away threats, and promote healing. This all happens fast and in ways we may never have been able to predict beforehand, says Dr. Gilbert from Harvard University. Or, put another way, "Maybe the chains don't get lighter but you get stronger." (Rabbi Harry Rosenberg)

Begin to focus on the future as soon as you are ready to help yourself heal. As Norman Mailer said, "Growth, in some curious way, I suspect, depends on always being in motion just a little bit, one way or another." Ultimately, you, and only you can seek out the nutrition to restore or rehabilitate and fortify yourself. (One young patient, whose current family life was indeed very emotionally deprived, called this "foraging" for her "vitamin supplements.")

Once you have defined your emotional state, it's important to start to try to effect some changes. Even if you do it in baby steps, try to find experiences that can move your life forward. Be sure to give yourself credit for each one of these steps, no matter how small they may seem to an outside observer.

Sometimes our tree needs to be pruned back in order to heal and to grow fuller. If you are overextended in an area that isn't giving you adequate nutrients – especially overextended in a False Self mode erected primarily to please others – sometimes you might need to prune back *a lot*. This can be very strenuous at first but the growth and new blossoming that you will enjoy will make it worthwhile. (I thank my friend Rev. Susan VandeKappelle for this metaphor. She shared it with me when she described her work during retreats with people who were in transition and had to make changes in the structure of their lives.)

We know that making changes in one's life takes gumption. In psychology, the Holms and Raye scale attributes stress points equally for both positive and negative changes. Especially after a crisis, stress hormones are high. Frequently one's choices feel confined to "fight or flight." But researchers know that being constricted to these two choices raises the chances of physical illness and narrows one's vision for the future.

If one chooses "flight," they may withdraw, shrink from opportunity, contract the development of themselves (Andrew Morrison), and surrender their souls to other people whom they allow to take control and make decisions for them.

If one chooses "fight," holding angrily onto a grievance can become more important than resolving the problem. Stress hormones continue to circulate, sometimes for generations. Did you ever see the movie *Avalon*? Generations of a family ceased speaking to one another after the siblings failed to wait to carve the turkey on Thanksgiving until the eldest brother was present. Nothing got resolved and toxic stress hormones were passed from generation to generation. The Yiddish language has a word for all this called *broiges*.

Although he might not have known the term, Rev. Bruce Teague was addressing the destructiveness of the *broiges* when he said, "To forgive one must also realize that everyone is human and prone to mistakes and misjudgment. You never get out of victimhood until you face your own flaws." Or, as Dave would say, you can't embrace a "you shouldn't have done that" until you can own your own "I shouldn't have done thats."

Both Dave and I feel that it is important to learn to *recharge* your energy and actively institute changes that provide you with a feeling of control and revitalization. If you can gain access to the needs, values and goals of your True Self, you are on your way! Your pilot light can begin to kindle and burn again.

It is easy to learn the tools. Using the Nutritional Food Group Pyramid, and most importantly, knowing that the needs on this pyramid are *valid* paves the way for the ability to actively find the food that's needed. This builds strength. When there has been some sort of a shame wreck, loss, or devastation, both adults and children can be taught to take back control of their lives. The key is being able to mobilize one's self, to know and satisfy one's needs, so that hope can prevail over moments of despair.

This is not "rocket science." All people – young or old – can be taught some form of gardening. They can learn to rescue the development of their flower by doing three things: actively *giving it the nutrients* it needs, *clearing away the rubble*, and *removing the toxins* that are interfering with its vitality and bloom.

Some people, in an attempt to overcome feelings of helplessness, take a detour. They gravitate toward addictive behaviors. For even drinking, gambling, or taking medications is *doing* something. It is an attempt to solve a problem, though it is indirect, and in the end, usually self-destructive. Dr. Lance Dodes has studied this phenomenon for 25 years and says:

"If one feels that they can't speak up, they may turn to addiction to manage a sense of helplessness and anger. It's

225

a compulsion to perform an action to try to do something to recover. Even though it has a positive motivation, because it is a displacement, it often does not have a desirable effect."

In addition, behaviors such as heavy drinking, overeating, promiscuity, compulsive shopping, and substance abuse, are the kind of action one takes when one feels trapped and enraged at not being able, or not knowing how, to take more constructive actions.

When you are in a state of flux or crisis, when something "shouldn't have happened," somebody "shouldn't have done that," or "life shouldn't have done that," the Psychological Nutritional Food Group Pyramid is useful. You should deal directly with your underlying feeling of weakness and nourish yourself. Good nutrition will help reactivate your feelings of vitality and bring back the passion for life.

Also, people who are well fed by nature offer nourishment to others. They can give affirmation, idealization and twinship to others who need it to feel alive – creating an even more vitalizing feedback loop for all. So, don't be shy. Do all you can to boost your own self-image. You can think of it as altruistic; for as Dave says, "Positive vibes are contagious; they activate others."

In terms of "altruistic self-boosting" I often wondered, how does an entertainer such as Dave keep himself so *up* that he can keep on so energetically uplifting so many people? And then I discovered that Dave is known for writing inspiring letters to himself. He advocates the healthy aspect of being one's own cheerleader and making an effort to remember one's own successes. People who are able to generate for themselves feelings of *authentic* self-enhancement are the ones who become the most altruistic and enhancing of others. And you can tell the difference between a person who has true self-esteem because they make other people feel good about themselves, while those who are using arrogance or grandiosity to compensate for or cover up low self-esteem almost always decrease the sense of well-being of those around them.

One technique of Dave's I particularly like is his program of empowerment. Again, taking a metaphor from biology, we can call this "shame inoculation." One of the best ways of doing this is, when you make a mistake, chant to yourself, "Shouldn't have done that." It's important that you chant this in the same sing-songy, smooth, non-harsh or judgmental intonation that Dave uses in all of his movies. Practice "I shouldn't have done thaaaaaat…"; "You shouldn't have done thaaaaaaat…"; or "That shouldn't have haaaaaaappened." If you chant this like a mantra it will come to you readily and automatically when you need it.

A patient of mine who had watched Dave's movie told me a story. He was having a very frustrating day trying to hang some curtain rods. He was standing on his bed, holding the rods way above his shoulders and above the window. He was trying to balance to the right and to the left and the rods were slipping off the screws. He was having a terrible time. Nothing was lining up correctly and his arms were getting tired. Suddenly, he slipped off the bed, the curtain rod falling on top of him. He not only tumbled down, but he fell onto an antique cloth Japanese screen that was next to bed dividing two rooms in his apartment. He heard a tearing sound and saw that a big hole had been made in it. Although he was alone, before he knew it the phrase that automatically came out of his mouth was "shouldn't have done thaaaaaaaat." He told me this story because he was amazed at how the phrase had "gotten into his blood."

This man was all alone when he said, "Shouldn't have done thaaaaaaaat" and was comforted by the mantra. But you will also find that when you say the phrase to someone else whom you might have offended, that there will almost always be a salutary effect. In everyday life, people are often more touched when you say you're sorry and admit the mistake than they would have been injured by what you did to them. Numerous examples are shown in the Dave series, where he can take embarrassing moments lightly, admit his error, and others then take his mistakes softheartedly.

The key is to remember is it's just a "shouldn't have *done*," and the deed is just an event. When episodes of "you shouldn't have done that" occur, try not to see it as a personal confirmation of your own "badness" or the "badness" of the other.

All Dave's movies are in fact about doings. We see Dave constantly toying with the struggle of whether he will be the victim or the hero, the aggrieved party or the disappointing dufus. When Dave fails, flops, faints, gets hooked on the crane, gets knocked over by a rush of water in a fire truck, falls over the edge of a hill, lands on a strange planet when his spaceship crashes, runs out of gas because he didn't fill the gas tank on his motorcycle, makes the submarine rise out of the water, runs over his father's car or dumps Becky in the garbage truck, his fate can go two ways: he can either become "done in" or survive. He can either quit in defeat or continue and thrive.

The way he *processes his thinking* after an "I shouldn't have done that," is what lets him *define himself* as a hero and not a victim.

No one is saying that defining oneself is easy to master, and no one is saying that this is an automatic process. In real life, it doesn't happen as quickly as it does for Dave in his movies. In real life it takes work, and in real life, the hurts and injuries are frequently far more threatening and complex.

But the principle is the same. You have to move your spirit and *do* something, whether or not you're in the mood. You can't wait for your spirit to move you. You have to seek out and grab the nutrients in the Psychological Nutritional Pyramid and find people, places, activities and contexts that can provide them.

Simply put, if there are no relationships or settings in your current life that can feed you what you need, it is *your* responsibility to "move to another garden" to find vitamin supplements. This does not necessarily mean giving up your primary garden (although it might) but you cannot give up your need for food. And, because you cannot deny these needs if you are to bounce back, it is incumbent upon *you* to make it your mission to forage for what you need.

I know a prominent physician who was lucky because her nutrients came to her. She was married for 20 years to another physician and was shocked when she found out that her husband was having an affair with his secretary. She told me, "I never would have expected this. I trusted him so fully. I was totally shattered." (He really "shouldn't have done that.")

She told me that she felt so emotionally wounded and devastated that she lay in bed, consumed with thoughts of dying – unable to move, and disbelieving that her life course had been altered so drastically. Within a few hours, her daughter, who was visiting from college, bounded into the room unexpectedly and asked her mother if she would accompany her to dinner. The doctor was astounded to feel the sudden rush of warmth that came over her like a wave. At that moment she saw herself through her daughter's eyes and became in touch almost instantaneously again with her own sense of worth and value as a person. She bounded out of bed, got "dressed up very well," as she described it, and she and her daughter went out to dinner together. Her sense of worthlessness evaporated and did not return again.

Right now, think more in detail about who and what you have put into your pyramid. This pyramid will remain precious to you as your "work in progress," your guide to self-restoration. Expect it to grow, evolve and change as you do, and as your life's journey progresses. If you are in a crisis, you will find out whether the people, activities and places that you have listed can be depended on as "food sources."

Anyone who has experienced a crisis such as divorce or a death in the family will tell you about the surprises they have faced in this regard – people that they never would have anticipated who have come forth to be supportive and helpful, and others who they were sure were true-blue friends who have remained nowhere to be seen.

The late Dr. Arlene Francis has said, "Troubles are the sieve with which we sift our acquaintances. Those too big to pass through are our friends."

# CHAPTER 10

## REFLECT ON YOUR OWN PYRAMID...
## YOUR SHELTER FROM HEAVY STORMS AND HURRICANES

Now it's time to concentrate more on your Psychological Nutritional Pyramid worksheet and to practice thinking about your own nutritional needs. You will find a blank pyramid to cut out and write on at the end of this book. Themes we have developed will be expanded upon in this chapter so that by the time you are finished, you should be fully equipped with most of what you need to know about "bouncing back." We will also provide additional case examples to expand your understanding.

As we have said, when we talk about the five Psychological Food Groups for the self, we are talking about what nourishment contributes to and fortifies the basic sense of strength and resilience of the self. What nutrition does one have to get from the environment in order to grow up feeling whole, healthy, and alive? How does one get that nutrition when there is a reversal and, therefore, a need to "bounce back"?

It's simple. Having these five core nutritional needs met will make one feel strong; not having them met will make one feel weak, shame-ridden, and vulnerable. Adults need to learn to be accountable for their needs and not be shy about saying, "I'm hungry" when their needs are not met. Adults must teach their children the same skill. The goal of health and happiness is to have a balanced diet of connectedness, mirroring, idealization, twinship and sparring experiences.

Success and resilience is about doing something to make (or re-make) these healthy nutritional choices. It is about being proactive in finding experiences or relationships that nurture, and nourish, along *all* of the five food groups and assembling a diet of experiences that provide the nutrition needed to stay strong or regain strength. Recognizing the *validity* of the needs is the key. As we acknowledge these needs as normal across all ages of the life span, we learn to be accountable to ourselves for trying to get our own needs met. We also realize the importance of providing these nutrients for our children and for encouraging verbalization of these needs within families.

We can expect that, at certain times in our lives, we will be hungry and binge on one or more of the food groups. Some terrible loss – such as the loss of a job or a mate, a death in the family, some drastic injury to our self-esteem or some huge disappointment – will weaken us. In these times of stress, we crave one or more of the food groups in the pyramid. A wise patient of mine said, "Life is such that you can never know if you've really survived until it's all over because we never know what's going to happen to us next!"

Just knowing and being able to label what nutrient it is that we are hungry for is half the battle. As adults, it is up to us to *name* these needs to make them known. The advantage of aging is that the longer you live, the more you know about yourself. It has been said that:

"We grow neither better nor worse as we get old, but more like ourselves."
(Editor and writer May Lamberton Becker)

So the more you know what your needs are, and where your hunger lies, the more you can manage them, because these needs are never outgrown.

Our needs are all there from birth until death in our same trusty Psychological Nutritional Pyramid. So, never let anyone tell you that you should "outgrow" any need at all. Bouncing back requires renouncing the natural feeling of helplessness and searching out the nutrients. This active attitude means we do not have to stay stuck in the role of the victim, or the villain. It means having a range and flexibility of choices far beyond the typical two of fight or flight.

If there has been deprivation in the food pyramid of psychological nutritional needs, especially during childhood, the individual will develop what psychologists call a "negative self-schema." This is just a fancy term to describe a negative self-image. He develops a belief system about what he is like in the world, and a strongly held expectation about how he will be experienced by others.

This "self-schema" is very subtle, and because it is so deeply ingrained in the person as an unquestioned *belief* it takes a lot of work to uncover it. I often use the image of a pair of glasses that each person wears – a pair of lenses, ground by early experience, so that we see our world and ourselves in a certain way. That is, we organize our perceptions of ourselves and our own world in certain ways, according to our past individual experiences.

People who grow up with environmental deprivation in nourishment on the nutritional pyramid develop ways of seeing themselves that persist throughout their lives and are often subconscious. They believe this perception is an unalterable reality. It becomes a sort of lens through which they look; their subjective point of view truly becomes their reality.

Anyone who has tried to "correct" someone else's strongly held sense of reality about themselves knows how difficult (to impossible) this can be.

If a person has a negative self-image it is very easy for them to have that self-image confirmed when they, themselves, make a mistake or when someone else fails them. People with "self-schemas" that cause them to believe that they are bad, worthless, unimportant, or unlovable have a difficult time being resilient. The reason for this is that they take a mistake they might make or a slight made by another as a personal reflection confirming their long-held negative view of themselves in the world. We have all known people who have a hard time bouncing back from a slight or injury, forgiving someone who has hurt their feelings, has taken offense when we didn't mean to hurt them, or who always feels like a victim. Tragically, there are now victims' groups that have banded together that are seeking revenge on other groups of people – groups that feel so injured that they feel legitimate in referring to themselves as victoterrorists.

Here's a rather dramatic illustration of poor resilience. A woman in my practice was having neck surgery. I was going to be out of town at the time. I said to her, "I'm very concerned about this surgery and how anxious you are about it.  I know you're very worried about the anesthesia.  I'm going to have you on my mind when I'm away. Would you please give me a call when you're back in your room? I'll be out-of-town and it will be very hard for me to telephone you. Just leave me a message on my answering service.  Just let me know you're OK and how it went.  I'll be thinking about you all day."

My patient never left me a message.  The next day, I returned to town and telephoned her.  She was enraged at me "How dare you tell me to call you," she said.  "If you really cared about how my surgery went, you would have found a way to call me.  I can't believe that you didn't call me."

Taken aback, and trying to center myself from the attack (because I knew I had been truly authentically concerned about her), I apologized.  After we had both calmed down, I asked her what this had meant to her, that I had not called her but instead had asked her to call me.  She said, "This is what it means to me.  Nobody ever extends themselves for me.  Nobody ever extends themselves to see how I am.  I'm always the one who extends myself for other people, and now you.  I thought that at least *you* could go out of your way to find out how *I* am, but once again, I had to wait for you.  It's just like the rest of my life.  Nobody ever extends themselves or goes out of their way for me!"

As you might imagine, this patient had had a very traumatic childhood, with an extremely self-centered mother whose needs she always had to make center stage.  The mother truly never went out of her way for her daughter.  Now, in her current life, my patient remains prone to believe that all situations will be the same way, including the one with me. Despite our longstanding relationship, her automatic expectation is that I, too, will consider her feelings as less important than my own agenda.

As you probably know from your own experience, it is very painful and frustrating to deal with a situation where your own motivation is interpreted so out of line with what you intended. This example illustrates how the lack of early mirroring had given this patient the sense that she wasn't important, wasn't worth seeking out, wasn't worth any effort to be paid attention to, and that if she was going to get any attention, she had to take the initiative.

Here is another example. A patient of mine told me that while he was in school, he was so used to being devalued and put down by the teachers, that he learned to expect being degraded as an everyday occurrence. He remembers one occasion when he was walking with two other students, with an Irish setter following 10 steps behind them. The teacher called to the dog, "Hey stupid!" and all three students automatically turned their heads toward their teacher, thinking that they had been called!

The point is that people who grew up deprived of nourishment of these basic needs develop ways of seeing themselves that persists throughout their lives, and often they are not aware of their self-schema until they come into analysis. But you can see evidence of it in the way they react to things, and in the way they comport themselves. The earlier the deprivation is on the pyramid, the more disturbed their reactions are. We all know of children deprived of the most basic food group of connectedness who exhibit difficulties, early on, in becoming attached and connected to caregivers. Children who are deprived of mirroring often starve for attention, throwing temper tantrums if they feel ignored, or becoming obsessed with capturing the limelight by becoming prodigies, entertainers or movie stars.

Sometimes people who are deprived of idealization supplies develop a compulsive need to attach themselves to important people. We've all seen "groupies," people who follow around one important person after another, feeling self-esteem only if they are attached to somebody they can see as important, or heroic. And, as I have mentioned, the scariest examples of people with unmet twinship needs are people who are vulnerable to being lured into joining cults. These are individuals who seem unable to exist unless they're going to an extreme of joining with people who think *exactly* as they do. There is no tolerance for difference at all. People who exhibit these symptoms clearly have had serious nutritional deprivation somewhere in the food group.

But it is important to always keep in mind that we all have multiple needs from the various psychological nutritional food groups *all through life*. The nutrients that children need in order to grow to be strong are exactly the same ones adults need in order to *remain* strong, to *regain* strength, or to retain flexibility and also *compassion*. I select the word compassion because it is the common sharing of these needs on the pyramid that makes us ultimately human and gives us the ability to "feel for" each other and to have empathy. Knowing that we all share the same needs allows us to help each other bounce back and encourages mutuality in relationships.

Some of us, because of earlier deprivations or even temperamental factors that we may not understand, have stronger needs in one sector of the pyramid than others, just as some people's metabolism may need more protein than others for unknown reasons. But the basic message here is, *never let anyone tell you that you should have "outgrown" any feeling.* It doesn't matter what the feeling is.

You are pre-wired to need people. The goal of mental health is achieving and maintaining healthy connection experiences, healthy mirroring experiences, healthy idealizing experiences, healthy twinship experiences, healthy sparring experiences – with your friends, your mate, your children, your co-workers, your boss, your ideas, your teammates or whoever you are in contact with. The goal is to not be subsumed by anybody, not be overwhelmed by anyone, not be dominated or submissive, but to be in *healthy, mutual relation.*

When one suffers a setback or a reversal, a crisis ensues, often with feeling of powerlessness. One clearly feels helpless when one has financial reversal, or reversal in one's physical health or condition. A reversal in a personal relationship or a reversal in one's profession can flatten one, "take the life" out of one or the "wind out of one's sails." It is at these times that people can succumb to all sorts of symptoms.

Symptoms are normal and indicate that something is wrong. The key is understanding them, naming the feelings and being able to *activate* oneself out of the sense of helplessness and victimhood. As Fred Shero, coach of the Philadelphia Flyers, has said, "Success is not the result of spontaneous combustion. You must set yourself on fire." Some people are blessed with a more resilient nature because they had a nourishing childhood environment, can resurrect themselves more easily and gracefully than others. But here is the key: both Dave and I share the belief that when life flattens you and you have to pull yourself up, all you need is *one person* to tell you it's possible. And that message is what this book is all about.

Unfortunately, in human life, relations with people and things do not always go smoothly – hence, the topic of this book: how to "bounce back." Everyone experiences reversals. All reversals evoke self-doubt, surges of depression, a sense of crisis and the ensuing challenge of revitalization. Setbacks in which life "shouldn't have done that" affect us all. Events, whether precipitated by one's self, by another, or just bad luck will cause pain, and pain causes both psychological and physical symptoms.

I once had a patient who told me about a story she had read as a child about a dog who wore a sign around his neck that said, "I am lovable and capable." The story was about how the sign kept getting marred, chipped, and cracked as the dog went through his adventures. Every day, the sign tried very hard to not fall apart. At night, while the dog was asleep, somehow magically the sign restored itself, and when the dog woke up, the sign became bright and shiny as if brand-new again. Now, self-restoration may not be as easy as the dog's magical sign, but there are some trusty guidelines that can be followed, to help put our lives back together after we have been "thrown about and injured."

Experts are now discovering that it can be months or years after a traumatic event before its full impact is felt. Disturbing stories are emerging among individuals who have been intimately involved (and even labeled as heroes) in rescue efforts, such as the 2002 Pennsylvania coal mine disaster, the 1995 Oklahoma City bombing, and Sept. 11, who have gone on to commit suicide, become alcoholics, or destroy themselves through gambling and other impulsive behaviors.

Bob Long, a surveyor who was credited with finding the nine trapped coal miners killed himself in June 2003. The year after he rescued four bombing victims in 1995, Terry Yeakey, an Oklahoma City police sergeant, committed suicide. Robert O'Donald, a paramedic, took his own life nearly eight years after playing a crucial role in saving baby Jessica McClure from a Texas well shaft in 1987. At least three New York men involved in rescue and recovery efforts have committed suicide since Sept. 11. Others have become trapped in alcoholism or other self-destructive behaviors such as gambling.

The reasons for some of these tragedies may never be known, but some are most likely due to the overwhelming challenge of being able to recover from the haunting memories of rescue efforts. In addition, "ordinary people" who are suddenly idealized and portrayed as heroes may not be able to integrate such sudden fame into their self-image. They are unprepared for the kinds of resentments and envies that such renown can bring, says Leo Braudy, a University of Southern California professor who wrote *The Frenzy of Renown: Fame and Its History*.

Since Sept. 11, 2001, the American Psychological Association has launched a "road to resilience" public education campaign to help people with both major crises and daily stressors. Bridget Murray summarizes the message of the 2003 APA convention by saying, "Resilience is not something we're born with, it is a set of learned behaviors and it takes strategizing to build." (APA Monitor, October 2003, p. 42) In order to move on after a traumatic event, one needs to take on for oneself what Carl Jung and his successors have described as the "basic functions of parenting": nurturing, protecting, empowering and initiating.

Dave and I have summarized the Psychological Nutrition Pyramid for you here so that you can cut it out and keep in a handy place (just as you would keep water or duct tape in preparation for a hurricane) – and with the same confidence that you *can* prepare, that your garden will survive, and that the storm *shall pass*. Now, follow along with us on your blank pyramid.

*Connectedness:* Think about people in your life who contribute to your sense of positiveness - people who are supportive of the nature and goals of your True Self and who enable you to thrive. We know that being with certain people can give you a sense of wholeness, happiness, energy and aliveness while being with others can make you feel drained, depleted, and fraught with a lingering self-doubt. In fact, there was even an article published in the Dec. 15, 1996, *New York Times* entitled "You Were Right in Saying Some People Make You Sick" that described the phenomenon whereby people actually are more inclined to become physically ill in the presence of certain people. (Do you have a cold or the flu right now?)

So, take this moment to list the people with whom you currently feel the most sense of connection. Also include those people with whom you have not maintained a relationship, but who have provided you in the past with a sense of connection and with whom you might someday want to reconnect. Keep these people on your "reserve" list.

*Mirroring:* We all need people who admire us for who we are. Find people who admire you for *you*, not for what you do or for whom you know. Don't be bashful; mirroring is a very healthy need. Ask yourself: "Do the people that I surrounded myself with now admire me for my True Self, or for my accommodation to what they need, that is for my caretaking functions?"

Mirroring does not even have to be verbal. The most profound mirroring of all comes from the sense of being heard, understood, kept in mind, and deeply listened to. The telling sign is that when we are exposed to people by whom we feel truly mirrored, we feel open, alive, relaxed, spontaneous, and unself-conscious.

*Idealization:* Re-evaluate your ideals. I knew a middle-aged man who was at the height of his career. He was experiencing an emotional crisis because he realized he had no time for his family and his wife kept joking about divorce. He was also developing symptoms of angina. This was a crossroads. He could either continue to stress himself with long hours, working at high intensity, making a lot of money, or he could re-evaluate his ideals, and decide whether his value system made it more important for him to make time for his family and his children. He shuffled the cards of life, so to speak, and left his high-pressure job, bought a house near a lake (that he loved), opened a business making and selling furniture (he had always loved carpentry), and finally had the flexibility to invest his time with his loved ones.

Take some time to assess the values that your True Self admires. In this process, think of people you might like to emulate and write down what makes them appealing.


*Twinship:* Think of someone who you think is a lot like you. Pick a twinship variable that means a lot to you. Consider making an effort to spend some time with this person or persons. Sometimes people who have suffered from cancer find sustenance in spending time with other cancer survivors. For others, that is the last thing that they want to do. In *There Goes a Roller Coaster*, Dave reconnects with the "child inside himself," by pulling away from the tedium of his business problems and reconnects with the child in himself by twinning with his son at an amusement park. The important thing is to use your creativity here. Find an aspect of someone that twins with you and vitalizes you, and make it a point to go be with him and enjoy it together.


*Sparring:* This is the least talked about Psychological Food Group because there is so much confusion between assertiveness and aggression. Also, people are overwhelmed with the aggression in our world and have lost an appreciation for their own need for sparring. (That is, until they go to Maine and want to crack open a lobster or fight with some crab legs.) But sparring can involve driving a golf ball onto the fairway or "whipping" a good friend on the tennis court, then enjoying a cold drink and a hot meal. It's a healthy way to burn off frustrations and undo a sense of helplessness. Use your pyramid now to fill in some options for healthy sparring, for some invigorating to and fro in your life. Maybe this will be something of a physical nature, or of an intellectual nature. But remember, you *need* some of this in your diet.

*Help Your Flower Begin to Bud:* Think about what *talents* or *skills* might be germinating underground that you may be able to further develop. These may be nascent skills such as an interest in art, music, writing or poetry, which you have dabbled in but never fully explored. Sometimes in times of crisis, when a vital aspect of one's world is removed, I have seen people begin to cultivate a "bud" of a talent or skill that they have newly cleared a path for. Through nurturing and developing this "bud," a whole new purpose for their lives has been created one that never would have emerged otherwise. A stunning example of this is J.K. Rowling, who, faced with a frightening lack of money, decided to take a chance to write down some stories that had been in her head. Hence, the Harry Potter books!

*Be Vigilant:* Keep away anything that could be toxic to your flower. Take some time in *solitude* and try to examine what self-schema your crisis may have activated. Did falling over the hill make you feel like a "doofus"? Did driving over your father's car make you feel like an "irresponsible son"? Did mistakenly scooping Becky into the garbage truck make you feel like a "lousy friend"?

The most serious damage of a "shouldn't have done that" crisis is the activation of a self-schema that lies dormant and of which we are typically unaware. And one of the most powerful roadblocks in a crisis is the negative self-schema that resurrects itself. Learn what *your* self-schema is. It could have been placed there by someone else, or you could have created it as a child to explain some disappointment in the nutrition of your own life.

The reason Dave is able to move so deftly beyond "I shouldn't have done that" is that he has no negative self-schema that gets activated and that he trips over. It's the *event*, and that's it! He moves on. No negative view of himself is confirmed.

If you find yourself stuck and unable to move beyond the phrase "shouldn't have done that," try, even if you need outside help, to uncover your core beliefs or whatever negative self-schema might be holding you back. You *can* control the effect of these beliefs on you, because they are only subjective. They are only *beliefs* you just *think* are *real* because you have believed them unquestioningly for so long.

You know that when you mistakenly cut someone off on the road, you are *not* saying to him, "I don't care about you," even if *he* subjectively perceives it that way. The goal is to try to develop "a new relationship with your difficulty, such that it is no longer a controlling factor in your life. What may seem like an intractable wound may even become a point of inspiration and deep understanding for you." (Philip Moffitt)

I thank Father Ed Czarnicki for pointing me to the wonderful story in the Old Testament called the Prayer of Jabez (1 Chronicles

4:9). In Hebrew, *jabez* means pain. Jabez' mother had named him Jabez because she had given birth to him in pain. Bruce Wilkinson, author of the book *The Prayer of Jabez*, says: "Not only did his name sound gloomy; everyone knew it spelled doom. For Jewish children, a name was taken as a prophecy of that child's temperament and destiny. From childhood on, Jabez would be a prisoner of pain."

Now ask yourself, "What desirable options have I never seriously considered simply because they didn't match up with my negative name?" Wilkinson advises saying a prayer: "Lord, what labels or attitudes have I attached to my life that might be limiting what you want to give me, who you want to make me, or what you want to do through me? Please show me."

You do not need to be defined by your self-schema or the happenstance of your prior childhood nutrition.

*Be Diligent about Tending Your Garden:* You can feed yourself now. Look at the pyramid you're filling in. Go for the banquet!

Most importantly, remember that your pyramid is always a work in progress; you can change your entries at any time.

That power of *revision* is the essence of resilience.

# CHAPTER 11

## SUMMARY

To summarize the big message in this little text: success is an attitude, not a fixed point of achievement, or even a permanent endpoint. Research has shown that setting a goal for success or even reaching that goal is an unreliable way of ensuring happiness (Gertner, 2003). This is for two reasons.

First, people accommodate to successful events. We are rarely as thrilled or happy with successful events as we predict we will be. Similarly, we are rarely as devastated by unhappy events as we expect to be.

Second, even when one has great success, one cannot predict what other factors might also be happening at that time that might mitigate against unencumbered feelings of euphoria. As an example, many envied the beauty, fitness, athletic accomplishment and wealth of the tennis players Venus and Serena Williams – that is, until the stars experienced the tragic murder of their older sister in September 2003.

No success happens in a vacuum, so it makes no sense to talk about success as an endpoint. Rather, an attitude of success is something that we can strive to maintain throughout all the ups and downs of our human existence.

When we look at so-called successful lives, we do not see what would look, on a graph, like an undisturbed rising line. Often there are episodes of falling, spells of drooping, periods of setback, discouragement, failure, or in spiritual terms, "dark nights of the soul."

Yet in successful children and in successful people, we see an ability to bounce back, self-restore, "dust themselves off," "get back on the horse," or whatever other metaphor we wish to use. We see an ability to activate and to try again. We see a personality unencumbered by adhesive feelings of shame; for shame has the strongest potential to bog down vitality and to put a damper on hope.

In people with a success attitude, we see a personality that the Rev. Robert Schuller describes as a "possibilitizer" – one that can recognize an opportunity because he can remain aware of what he values and what is important to his True Self. This resilient person has been able to sustain the discipline and enthusiasm to pursue options with optimism in situations where others may focus only on their own defeat. All of the above elements comprise what Dave and I have termed the **P.R.I.D.E. Factor**™.

Burton Hills wrote, "Happiness is not a destination. It is a method of life." Success is an attitude about trying and bouncing back. Resilience is about knowing how to employ the Psychological Nutrition Pyramid and about finding or re-finding one's unique purpose in life.

Hurt and disappointment are a normal part of life. As humans we are all subject to reversals, defeats and setbacks. We fail ourselves. People fail us. Life fails us. The difference between people who continue to thrive and those who remain in the defeat mode is whether or not they are eventually able to mobilize the resources available inside themselves, as well as in their outside and interpersonal world and move forward. Then, "problems become challenges to overcome, not simply grievances on which to dwell." (Luskin, p.45)

Dave's mantra "Shouldn't have done that" offers a jumping-off point for how one can learn to bounce back when something unwanted happens. It acknowledges that something unfortunate or even bad *has indeed* happened: "*I* shouldn't have done that." "*You* shouldn't have done that." "*Life* shouldn't have done that." There *is* accountability – a mistake is made, a lesson learned. But as the movies portray, there is no ensuing hopelessness, helplessness, unending grievance, indelible shame or withdrawal of love.

Dave's movies, as well as his philosophies, embody hope. The injury is taken seriously; learning occurs from it. But the misfortune or tragedy does not become the defining aspect of the story. "Shouldn't have done that" does not *excuse* the injury. It does not deny that there has been an injury either to the self or the other. It does not overlook the effect of the injury or condone it. But it offers the possibility of not having to stay stuck in the injury or resonate indefinitely from it. As Dave puts it, you must be able to at least consider visualizing a place of "unstuckedness."

Harvard University psychologist Daniel Gilbert has done research which shows that people anticipate that an event ahead of them will have a larger and more enduring impact on them than it really does – whether it's for good or ill – and he has studies to substantiate this. Gilbert adds that in pursuing happiness "we should have more trust in our own resilience and less confidence in our predictions about how we all feel. We should be a bit more humble and a bit more brave." (*USA Today*, Dec. 9, 2003)

Throughout this book, Dave and I have tried to offer a model for helping people learn how to move out of being trapped in shame, guilt, anger and hurt. We agree with Marcel Proust that:

"The real voyage of discovery consists not in seeing new landscapes,
but in having new eyes."

In fact, recent research says that some people gain *pleasure* from mastering new experiences and coping with repairing things that have gone *wrong* (Emde 1991). Other authors have substantiated that the ability to find creative solutions to negative events can actually bring pleasure (Folkman and Moskowitz 2000). I think Christopher Reeve was trying to capture the grit and arousal involved in surmounting difficulties when he said, "You either decide to stay in the shallow end of the pool or you go out into the ocean."

We are promoting the idea that resilience and empowerment are generated by the mobilization of the Psychological Nutrition Pyramid, and through being open to using creative ways to restore one's sense of self and vitality. Of course, there will be a period of "down time" to digest and understand the trauma and feelings of helplessness, injury, or loss. There may be a need for coasting and regrouping. However, to have a model at hand to help one move forward gives hope for being able to do something active towards resuscitating old dreams or creating new ones to pursue.

By reflecting on the needs of your True Self and on the places you could go to get connection, affirmation, idealization, twinship, and sparring, you can jump-start your future and begin to reignite your sense of self-esteem and self-worth. Once this sense of vitality begins to kindle, it can heat up more and more. One does not have to remain suffocated in shame, vengeance, victimhood, vindication, shaming-back, or humiliation. If one is going to light up one's "attitude of success," one must realize that much of life is about re-equilibrating one's sense of self in relation to an event of life, or to what someone or something else has done. Surviving and thriving is about flexibility – flexibility to find one's nutrition and to redefine one's purpose.

The message in Dave's movies is that failure and misfortune do not have to represent the end of the game. When a pilot light has gone out, or nearly goes out, we need to take responsibility for putting in good fuel. We give special attention to stoke the pilot light and protect it from wind, to get our fires burning again. As Dave says, "You are the only person whom you must ask permission to make these changes."

Within this model of actively getting in touch with the needs of the True Self, we must define our purpose, and make sure we have all the nutrients from the Psychological Food Groups. Only then can we begin to stoke the fires, re-stimulate our vitality, get the juices flowing again, and come to feel invigorated and alive – mentally, physically, emotionally, and spiritually. Otherwise, to paraphrase Dr. John Hunter (c.1700), our lives are in the hands of any rascal who chooses to annoy us.

In summary, I believe that much of the fascination of Dave's movies is that they entrance people by the repetitive message that both a person's self and his relationships can be disrupted and then repaired. The building can fragment, so to speak, and then be made to pull together again. There can be slights, hurts, disappointments, angers, losses, irritations and blow-ups (literally!) and the result does not have to be a "deal breaker."

Dave and Becky are refreshing characters. Despite scraps and setbacks, they hold no longstanding grievances or personal shame wrecks. They don't carry grudges or lingering resentments. They are not bogged down by either their own failures or their reactions to being failed. And, no matter what happens, the core reason they can return to an attitude of such grace and happiness is that inside themselves they can hold on to a sense of value of both themselves and the other.

Provision of the elements of the Five Psychological Food Groups early on in life gives children the likelihood of having more resilience in the face of life's "shouldn't have done thats." But no matter what our childhoods have been, all of us are subject to unexpected negative events that can set us back, and all of us have the responsibility to ourselves to self-restore or rebound to benefit our lives and the lives of others. Using the Psychological Food Group Pyramid requires some time, effort and personal commitment, but it is possible and it will make you stronger.

Using the pyramid will help you visualize and put into words your own needs and help you start to think about how they can be fulfilled so that you can begin to nurture, strengthen and revitalize yourself. Not only will you feel validated in this mission, but you will begin to redefine a purpose, goal and meaning for your life. The momentum will begin to build.

Although rebuilding one's life takes work, the task is not monumental. This is because the pyramid is composed of basic human needs – things you can "get in an ordinary grocery store," so to speak. They are needs that can be fulfilled if you are willing to take action. Remember, in all of Dave's movies, he faces the *choice* about whether to be the victim or the hero. And, as so many of the stories in this book illustrate, so do we all. Whether we find ourselves in a pickle, or a serious life tragedy, we have choices about how to build ourselves up and get out of our weakened state.

We trust that the concepts in this book will be helpful to you when you take a tumble in love or work. Most of all, we hope that your life will be blessed with very few of these tumbles, or at least that the tumbles you do suffer will not be abnormally frequent or unduly severe. But when they do occur, we hope you will pick up this book again or inspire yourself by watching one of Dave's movies. Above all, remember:


"Be kind, for everyone you meet is fighting a hard battle." (Plato)


In conclusion, I would like to quote a clergywoman who was imprisoned for demonstrating against killings that she felt were inhumane and unfair. In an interview she said:


"I don't fear going to prison. I don't fear loss of freedom

to move about. I don't even fear death. The fear the fills me is not having lived hard enough, deep enough, and sweet enough, with whatever gifts God has given me."

— Dominican Sister Carol Gilbert, age 55

Sister's words are true to the words of **P.R.I.D.E.**™. As partners in human condition, what else, dear friends, can we ask of life?

With affection to all,

from your comrades in living,

Dave Hood & Carol Munschauer, Ph.D.

### Remember the P.R.I.D.E. Factor™

The principles expressed in this book can be summarized in Dave's and my **P.R.I.D.E. Factor**™.

Here is a handy reference guide. Cut it out and use it at those times in your life when "I shouldn't have done that," "You shouldn't have done that," or "Life shouldn't have done that" events occur – those times when you need to rely on the specifics of the **P.R.I.D.E. Factor**™ to promote and preserve your resilience.

### POSITIVITY:

1. Take time to breathe, rest, re-center, refocus, or regroup. Decide when to change gears and be proactive.
2. Jump-start your life and move forward. This is the essence of positivity.

3. Recognize the injury; accept that it happened, allow the emotions that are experienced.

4. Name the specific feeling evoked. Especially if it is shame, acknowledge it to yourself; try to share the feeling with at least one other person.

5. Reflect on what the specific injury means to you. Does it activate a previous "negative self-schema"?

6. Accept that the event was "bad," but separate the event from the person.

7. Make every effort to not feel ashamed for a mistake or embarrassed for feeling hurt and to learn from the injury. Having such strength is an example of others and is the beginning of moving forward with life's new adventures.

8. Try to envision a *new dream*. Remember the adage: "Two prisoners looked out of their window bars. One looked down and saw mud. One looked up and saw the stars."

## RESILIENCE:

1. Remember that an event, even a negative one, can be a starting point for beginning a new dream. Chant Dave's mantra "I shouldn't have done that," or extend it to "You shouldn't have done that" or "Life shouldn't have done that."

2. Turn on your own "starter button," "Fake it until you make it," or "Whistle in the dark." This is Dave's advice, because he believes that there are times when every successful person has to *act* as if he is doing well even though he's not fully back "in sync." Beginning to try to self-motivate and build

confidence can promote an internal feeling of success that often extends, in a feedback loop, to external success.

3. Resist creating a "grievance story" if someone did something bad to you or life did something bad to you.

4. Remember that grievance stories sap strength and that being unable to forgive correlates highly with disease and premature death.

5. Practice positive self-talk. Say things to yourself that build up your own sense of success or well-being, such as "I think I can" (like *The Little Engine That Could*), or as Dave has said, "I'm not afraid of heights!" or "I'm a good monster truck driver!" or "I love to shovel!"

6. Give yourself prompts, such as the colloquial expressions:
"Let it run off you like water off a duck's back."
"This too shall pass."
"Don't get into a pissing contest with a skunk."
"He hurt me, but I must consider the source."
"Where there's a will there's a way."

7. Use your imagination to raise your Vitality Pulse. Look for something you can work at that you love or a love relationship you can work at. Find your own metaphor to keep track of your VP.

8. Put this motto on your refrigerator: "Nothing is lost by trying – the big loss is just sitting back and not doing anything." (Father Dan Fink)

9. If you cannot reach a stage of being proactive, seek help from a friend or a professional.

## INTEGRITY:

1. Examine yourself to know what your *own* value system is and stay true to it.

2. "Follow the grain in your own wood." (Howard Thurman, clergyman)

3. Examine your life to understand what the needs of your True Self are, and be consciously aware of balancing the needs of your True Self with the needs of others.

4. Respect what *you* feel, what your needs are or what *your* child feels. Be aware of your pulls to accommodate; and when you choose to do so, factor in the price.

5. Concentrate on creating a purpose for your life or changing the purpose you previously had.

6. Remember who you are, not just what you did, so that your sense of worth comes from inside and so that you are not defined by random events or by mistakes that you happen to make.

7. Retain your positive self-schema. If you can't do so, get help from a friend or professional.

8. Resist being the recipient of someone else's judgment. This might only cause a sense of shame and helplessness, which is the antithesis of empowerment.

9. Remember the motto of Alcoholics Anonymous: "What *you* think of me is none of my business."

## DISCIPLINE:

1. Take responsibility yourself for getting your psychological nutritional needs met by focusing on filling in and revising your Psychological Nutrition Pyramid.

2. Take an honest and meticulous inventory of your nutritional supplies, or your potential supplies, even if you must venture beyond your current boundaries.

3. Stay centered on perceiving "shouldn't have done that" episodes as *events* to be mastered and not as end points.

4. Make positive efforts to shed feelings of shame before it leeches onto you "like scales of fish which overlap upon each other" (Hildelore Lahvas Duffy).

5. Remain in touch with your own goals and values and your own unique capabilities. Stay true to the values that are dear to your heart.

6. Be prepared to press the envelope of your own abilities by extending yourself into areas that catch your imagination and intrigue you.

7. Be a "possibilitizer" (Rev. Robert Schuler). When a creative thought appears, use your energy to nurture it and push it forward. Don't let it pass you by!

8. Focus on the process of success, *not the goal* or the product. Remember that a goal is achieved through gradual steps and through "ups and downs." Assume that there will be failures. "Even if you faint, fall, or fail, it is not finished; all is redeemable." (Dominican friar Sam Mattarazzo)

## ENTHUSIASM:

1. Use your fantasies and think BIG.

2. Study the lives of people you admire.

3. Believe in people who believe in *you.*

4. Keep close touch with your Vitality Pulse. Follow your joy and stay in touch with the thoughts and activities that stimulate your energy and make you feel invigorated. (These can vary widely from cuddling a baby in an intensive care unit, to watching a beautiful sunset, to listening to music, to having a conversation with an empathic friend.)

5. Don't be afraid to "prune." Eliminate activities and people that drain your energy or make you sick, or goals that are not your own. Use your trusty garden clippers.

6. Remember that when you, yourself, are enthusiastically full of the **P.R.I.D.E. Factor**™, you will be fertilizer for other people. You will help them grow, flourish and develop. Serve your children a banquet of the Five Psychological Food Groups. You will feel well fed yourself, and you will thrive as you watch those close to you develop into the beautiful flower that lies dormant within them.

*Bon Appetite!*

# The Psychological Nutrition Pyramid ™

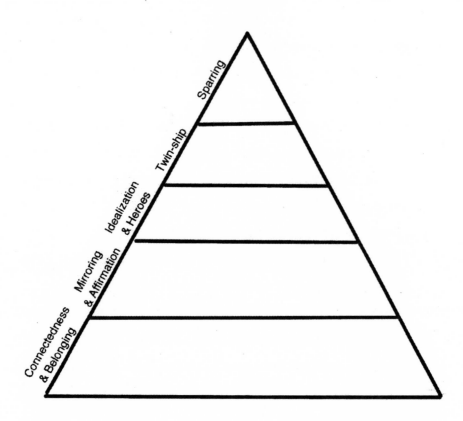

# APPENDIX

The success attitude is also about being informed enough to know when to get help. There are a few signs to be aware of that would indicate that your self is on overload that you most likely will not be able to handle by yourself or even by talking with a friend. These emergency signals mean that you need professional help in addition to using the pyramid model.

If you find yourself having frequent and uncontrollable rages, this is an indication that your sense of self-esteem is vulnerable and that your "nutritional needs" are in serious deprivation. This is most likely a situation that you cannot take care of on your own, or with the help of a friend, because your perspective on your self-worth is probably skewed. You are having a problem metabolizing some psychological foods right now and you need professional help.

In addition, if you find yourself overusing substances such as alcohol or drugs (prescription or otherwise), or relying on activities such as gambling or sexual acting-out in order to achieve the feeling of specialness, vitality or empowerment, you need to seek professional assistance. A good therapist can help you before the side effects of some of these behaviors can cause rocks to fall on your flower and maybe injure it permanently.

It is important to note that these behaviors are symptoms and not illnesses. Your psyche is using emergency measures to raise your self-esteem and get your attention. Your flower is desperately screeching for help. Although these measures may be working in the short term, the danger is that they can have long-term negative repercussions in your own life and for others in your garden.

Part of having a healthy success attitude is being able to locate a qualified person with whom to connect who can professionally assess the state of your self and the locations and depth (the roots) of your hurts and injuries. This compassionate assessment will help you begin to heal.

And as you are healing on the inside, you will naturally be able to relinquish these symptoms because you will no longer have the need for them. A good resource to look for professionals is the American Psychoanalytic Association (www.apsa.org/members/olroster.htm) or look for members of the American Psychological Association at www.apa.org

In addition, the American Psychological Association is currently focusing on a public education campaign about resilience. Information about this campaign is on the Web at www.apahelpcenter. org/resilience

For information on Dave Hood or his works visit: www. davemovies.com

CPSIA information can be obtained at www.ICGtesting.com
Printed in the USA
BVOW021551201112

306050BV00002B/3/A